The Success Archetype

How Wealth Follows Hidden Psychological
Patterns: An Investigational Analysis

Jessica Jameson

Magnetic Success

Copyright © 2025 by Jessica Jameson

All rights reserved. No part of this publication may be reproduced, stored in a retrieval system, or transmitted in any form or by any means—electronic, mechanical, photocopying, recording, or otherwise—without prior written permission of the publisher.

Jessica Jameson / Magnetic Success
Chicago, IL

Publisher's Note: This book is a work of non-fiction. It is based on the author's research, study, and interpretation of psychological, symbolic, and financial concepts. While every effort has been made to ensure accuracy, the information presented is for educational and informational purposes only and should not be construed as financial, legal, or psychological advice. Readers are encouraged to consult qualified professionals regarding personal decisions in these areas.

Research and Sources: The author has drawn upon published works in psychology, depth psychology, archetypal studies, and publicly available accounts of individuals and events for educational and analytical purposes. References to historical figures, public personalities, or case examples are for illustrative and educational use only. Interpretations, analyses, and conclusions are solely those of the author and do not represent endorsements or affiliations with the individuals, organizations, or sources mentioned.

Limit of Liability / Disclaimer of Warranty: The author and publisher make no representations or warranties with respect to the accuracy, applicability, fitness, or completeness of the contents of this work. They disclaim any warranties (express or implied) of merchantability or fitness for a particular purpose. Neither the author nor the publisher shall be liable for any loss or damages, including but not limited to special, incidental, consequential, or other damages, arising directly or indirectly from the use or reliance upon the information contained in this book.

Fair Use and Citation Notice: Certain excerpts, quotes, and references in this book are used for educational, research, and commentary purposes and are believed to fall under the principles of fair use. Any trademarks, brand names, or public figures referenced are used for illustrative purposes only and do not imply endorsement or affiliation.

Disclaimer: This book is for educational and informational purposes only. The content reflects the author's research and interpretation of psychological, symbolic, and financial concepts and is not intended as legal, financial, or psychological advice. The author and publisher (Magnetic Success) are not responsible for any actions or outcomes resulting from its use.

Edition and Version Note: The concepts, strategies, and insights presented in this book are current as of 2025. Changes in laws, regulations, or professional standards may affect the applicability of the content over time.

Author's Note: This book represents the author's original synthesis and interpretation of Jungian psychology as applied to wealth, success, and symbolic transformation. While it draws upon established research and published works, the perspectives, connections, and applications are unique to the author's analysis.

All trademarks, brand names, and copyrighted material referenced in this book belong to their respective owners and are used for educational and illustrative purposes only.

Published by Magnetic Success

© 2025 Jessica Jameson

Book Layout © 2017

The Success Archetype / Jessica Jameson
ISBN 979-8-9930377-0-7 (pbk)

To my family, whose love and unwavering support have made this journey possible; your presence in my life is my greatest inspiration. To my editor, whose guidance went far beyond the page—your advice and contribution were truly priceless. And to every individual who has faced financial challenges or struggled with success—may this book remind you that alignment is the secret to fulfillment.

Que este libro les recuerde que, sin importar las circunstancias, la grandeza está al alcance de quienes se atreven a creer en sí mismo.

CONTENTS

INTRODUCTION:
The Man Who Mapped The Invisible………..…..01

CHAPTER 1:
The Hidden Code Of Wealth……………..…....…11

CHAPTER 2:
Is It Really Just Coincidence?................................41

CHAPTER 3:
Defining The Hidden Pattern................................65

CHAPTER 4:
Breaking Financial Limitations……………….83

CHAPTER 5:
The Power Of Symbolism In
Financial Mastery...101

CHAPTER 6:
The Psychological Laws Of
Success And Failure..117

CHAPTER 7:
The Real Science Of Wealth Creation...............137

CHAPTER 8:
The Code Of Wealth: Aligning Action
With Intuition...153

CHAPTER 9:
Archetypes In Action And Rewiring
Your Mind For Financial Success........................165

CHAPTER 10:
Wealth, Power, And The Shadow:
Overcoming Psychological Barriers.....................179

CHAPTER 11:
Wealth Attraction Through Energy
And Frequency..195

CHAPTER 12:
Archetypal Analysis Of Wealthy Individuals..207

CHAPTER 13:
The Archetypal Wealth Integration Model..219

CHAPTER 14:
Living The Success Archetype..............................231

REFERENCES..................................……......237

ABOUT THE AUTHOR 241

INTRODUCTION

The Man Who Mapped The Invisible

Before we begin, let me introduce you to a man whose fingerprints quietly touch every page of this book. A man who never wrote a single word about wealth and, yet, whose psychological genius has everything to do with it. His name is Carl Gustav Jung. Jung was a Swiss psychiatrist, born in 1875, who dared to suggest that the human psyche is far more expansive than we had ever imagined. He believed that beneath our conscious thoughts lived an entire subterranean world, what he called the unconscious, which was a place where our fears, desires, dreams, and inherited patterns quietly influence every choice we make. Jung didn't stop there. He also proposed that we are all connected by something deeper than genes or geography: the collective unconscious, a shared field of symbolic meaning that holds the wisdom of humanity's psychological evolution.

Why does this matter in a book about wealth? Because your money story—which includes your habits, fears, self-worth, success patterns, and even your financial ceiling— is not just personal. It is psychological, archetypal, and generational. It is the echo of beliefs you may never have consciously chosen but still find yourself living out. Jung gave us the tools to name those echoes, to face the shadow, and to reclaim power from the very patterns that once kept us stuck.

This book is not based on surface-level success formulas. It is an investigation into the invisible architecture of wealth. It is for those who sense that no amount of strategy can override a psyche still tethered to scarcity. It is for those who are ready to go deeper. Jung showed us that transformation doesn't happen through information alone, but it happens when we meet the archetypes within us. It happens when we integrate the abandoned parts, and when we choose, moment by moment, to live not from our conditioning but from our wholeness. So, while Jung never wrote about money in the literal sense, his entire body of work provides a profound foundation for a new kind of wealth: one rooted not just in income, but in identity. What follows in these chapters is not just a book. It is a map through the inner terrain of your financial psyche that is guided by the timeless principles of Jung, reimagined through the lens of modern-day sovereignty, contribution, and self-mastery.

The Success Archetype

I've always been fascinated by the inner workings of the human mind. Long before I even knew what the term psychology meant, I found myself wondering why people behaved the way they did or what motivated them, what held them back, and how their internal worlds silently shaped the outcomes they experienced in life. Over time, that curiosity evolved into something more specific. I became deeply interested in those who seemed to navigate life with a kind of ease, effortlessly attracting wealth and opportunity. Why did some individuals thrive while others who were equally intelligent and capable simply remained stuck in cycles of struggle?

From a young age, I found myself observing the success of others, especially when it came to wealth, and asking the question that would follow me into adulthood: How is it that some people seem to live in effortless abundance, while others struggle endlessly, with little to nothing to their name?

My relationship with money began taking shape early in life. I was raised by a single mother who, from my perspective, never quite had enough. For years, I believed wealth was purely generational that was inherited or passed down through family lines. But that belief began to unravel as I looked more closely at the world around me. Today, many individuals who hold millionaire or even billionaire status are the first in their families to do so. These are self-made stories or even outliers in the traditional narrative of wealth.

But that raised a deeper question: How did they do it? I don't mean that just in the technical sense or investments. But how do they do it psychologically? What internal shifts had to take place for these individuals to break generational cycles and align with such extraordinary levels of success? What patterns of belief, identity, or emotional resonance allowed them to open the door to wealth that others unknowingly keep shut? These questions catapulted me into a personal investigation, one that led me to take a deep dive into the psychological components of success and the hidden forces that shape our relationship with wealth. Those early years of my life planted a seed deep in the mind that would grow, evolve, and eventually drive me to explore the truths behind wealth, success, and even scarcity. I came to realize that unlocking wealth isn't just a matter of numbers or luck. There's much more to it. It's psychological, symbolic, alignment and, most of all, it's deeply personal.

Today, my understanding of wealth has radically transformed, but that transformation didn't happen overnight. With every new job, financial opportunity, or unexpected raise, the conversation about money resurfaced. Each experience challenged beliefs I didn't even know I held, gradually forcing me to confront and rewrite the internal narrative I carried regarding wealth.

I wrote this book from an investigative lens and shaped it with a personal desire to understand. My efforts were fueled by insatiable curiosity and informed by years of observing those who had achieved extraordinary levels of financial success. What began as a simple question about wealth turned into a much deeper exploration of human behavior, unconscious programming, and what I now recognize as the psychological architecture of success. Over time, I noticed patterns or common threads running through the habits, belief systems, and mindsets of those who not only created wealth but also sustained it.

What I discovered—and it has been echoed by countless thought leaders, psychologists, and financial experts—is this: wealth does, indeed, begin in the mind. But unlike many approaches that only scratch the surface, my investigation led me far beneath it. I wasn't just interested in how people became successful. I wanted to understand why they stayed that way, and why so many others did not.

My research uncovered complexities that get to the root cause of actions and above all results. Success and wealth is something that has been debunked but on the surface level. My investigation goes deeper into what I now recognize as hidden codes. These codes are repeating patterns of thought, emotion, and behavior that directly correlate with unconscious beliefs and internal archetypes. They silently shape our financial reality, influencing everything from our ability to generate income to how we receive it, and most importantly multiply it.

As I began to investigate further into the mind inclusive of the facets of the subconscious and the conscious inner workings, I came across the work of Jung, a pioneering Swiss psychologist and psychiatrist, best known as the founder of analytic psychology. His work developed, in part, as a response to Sigmund Freud's theories, expanding our understanding of the psyche to include spiritual and symbolic dimensions.

Jung introduced key psychological concepts such as introversion and extraversion, universal archetypes, and the collective unconscious which is a shared layer of the human mind shaped by ancestral experience. His ideas have had a lasting influence not only in psychology and psychiatry but also in other related fields in literature.

As I delved deeper into my investigation, I began to see how wealth and the embodiment of it could be mapped onto the psychological frameworks introduced by Jung. Particularly, his teachings on individuation, shadow work, and the language of symbolism became essential keys in decoding what I now refer to as wealth psychology and the success archetypes. These archetypes or internal blueprints that govern behavior reveal themselves in subtle but powerful ways: in how we interpret financial synchronicities, in our inherited money beliefs, and even in how we respond to risk, reward, and opportunity.

Real-world success stories aren't just fueled by ambition; more often, they are expressions of deep psychological alignment between intention and behavior. Through this lens, even the self-sabotaging patterns we often ignore or mislabel as procrastination can be traced back to unintegrated aspects of the self. Jung's work on the subconscious, particularly shadow integration, shows us that true transformation isn't just possible but it's also essential. Symbols, once considered abstract or mystical, become powerful tools for reinforcing new beliefs and meaningful change. Behavioral finance, once confined to data and spreadsheets, becomes deeply personal when we uncover the emotional roots behind our decisions.

The path to wealth, I've come to understand, isn't solely about strategy or hard work. It's about merging mindset with manifestation as well as aligning conscious action with subconscious intention. It's about cultivating intuitive financial decision-making, mastering where we direct our energy, and applying cognitive rewiring techniques that create lasting change.

Ultimately, my investigation has led me to one profound conclusion: Wealth is a psychological state before it ever becomes a financial one. Lasting abundance doesn't begin with what we do, but it begins with who we believe we are. In the pages ahead, we'll explore the unseen forces that govern our financial behavior as well as belief systems you may not even realize you inherited. In addition to this we will explore in depth the unconscious patterns that quietly shape your ability to attract and grow wealth.

This book is written to inform; it's designed to help you align and transform. The tools suggested in the pages ahead are designed to uncover your hidden beliefs that may be keeping you financially stuck and to help rewire them at their roots. Whether you've hit a ceiling in your financial growth or you're just beginning to question the narrative you've been handed about money or success, you're exactly where you need to be. Here, you'll learn how to decode your unique success archetype, work with your shadow, and align your financial reality with your highest internal potential.

Because here's the truth: much of what we believe about money isn't truly ours. It's inherited and, essentially, passed down through our families. Other times it is embedded in our cultures, shaped by religion, and echoed in the collective stories society tells about what's possible and what's not.

Jung referred to this deeper layer of shared belief as the collective unconscious which is an invisible blueprint of archetypes, instincts, and thought patterns that live beneath our conscious awareness yet govern much of our behavior. When it comes to money, many of us are unknowingly operating from collective programs rooted in scarcity or even fear. We follow inherited scripts that were never ours to begin with and yet define how much we allow ourselves to earn.

To change our external results, we must first illuminate these unconscious drivers. We must step outside the narratives we didn't choose and reclaim the inner authority we've unknowingly given away. If wealth truly begins in the mind, then we must begin the transformation process by examining the invisible architecture shaping it. This means investigating the beliefs, emotional patterns, and generational imprints most people never think to question.

CHAPTER ONE

The Hidden Code Of Wealth

"Until you make the unconscious conscious, it will direct your life and you will call it fate."

—Carl Jung, Collected Works, Volume 8:

Believe it or not, wealth doesn't begin in your bank account. It doesn't start with a raise or an inheritance. Even if you have the best viral business idea, this still doesn't mean your wealth will automatically take off. Based on my research and deep inquiry, I've come to believe that true, sustainable wealth, the kind that transforms lives and echoes across generations, begins in the hidden architecture of the mind.

When I was growing up, there were virtually no conversations in our home about money. It simply wasn't a topic on the table. Like many children raised in working-class or financially limited households, I learned about money through the public school system, where it was presented in mechanical, transactional terms and never as a tool for freedom or transformation.

There were no lessons on how wealth was created, and certainly none on the psychological or emotional relationship we develop with it. As a young adult, I began forming my own beliefs about money, many of which seemed logical on the surface, but over time, revealed themselves as unsustainable.

One of the earliest beliefs I adopted was that saving every dollar was the key to financial freedom. In my mind, this meant working hard, living modestly, avoiding risk, and trusting that, one day, all this discipline would result in abundance. Eventually, I had to ask: was this really a wealth-building mindset? Or was it a fear-based survival mechanism? My family lived in neighborhoods teetering just above the poverty line, and later, we transitioned into a modest working-class area.

Even in this supposed upgrade, I noticed a pattern: people worked tirelessly and saved diligently, yet didn't seem to make significant financial progress. They were surviving but not thriving and, if you looked closer, there was an unspoken belief operating under the surface: that money had to be hoarded, or it would disappear. Every dollar saved was a form of safety, not a step toward expansion.

Eventually, I realized that, while saving is responsible, it is not a generative wealth strategy. It is a defensive one. Saving doesn't multiply wealth; it preserves what already exists. It is rooted in the fear of loss, not the vision of abundance.

Fast forward to my college years, where I adopted another common belief: that working multiple jobs would eventually lead to wealth. Eventually, that was the belief that so many of us clung to. After all, more hours meant more pay, right? But this model of trading time for money had a hard ceiling. The return on energy invested didn't compound. I watched friends work internships, part-time jobs, and maintain full course loads, all while chasing the mirage of financial freedom. They weren't building wealth; they were running in place. It was a model designed for survival, not liberation.

After college, my focus shifted again. I chased success the traditional way, by working on tasks above my pay grade and hoping to network my way up the corporate ladder. I bought into the idea that, if I just got the right title and the right recognition, then wealth would follow. Sound familiar?

At a certain point, I paused and asked a deeper question. Many individuals wanted to acquire lasting wealth. They were following the same formula of work harder and climb higher. Why, then, were so few people wealthy? What did successful people know that the rest of us didn't know? These types of questions led me down an unexpected path. I stopped reading books about money and started reading books about the human mental faculties. For months, I immersed myself in the different facets of psychology, inclusive of human behavior and the subconscious. And the deeper I went, the more I began to see a pattern emerge. It was one that most financial experts weren't really talking about.

The truly wealthy, the ones who weren't just rich on paper but expansive in presence, weren't operating from hustle. They weren't chasing success externally. They were running a different operating system entirely. It was one that was rooted not in external validation but in internal alignment. They had rewired their beliefs and emotional patterns to support wealth. They weren't just managing money, but they were also embodying a different relationship with it. They had cracked a code that wasn't written in financial literacy textbooks but was embedded deep within their psychology. And that's where the concept of wealth psychology enters.

Before we can unlock the hidden code of wealth, we need to understand the invisible force shaping our financial reality: wealth psychology. Wealth psychology is the study of how our thoughts, emotions, and unconscious beliefs about money influence our financial behaviors and outcomes. This goes far deeper than budgeting spreadsheets or even investment strategies. It's about uncovering the mental and emotional frameworks we've inherited and rarely question. It examines the identities we construct around our worth, success, and what we believe is financially possible for us.

Whether we realize it or not, we all carry internal scripts about money. These scripts are rarely written by us consciously. Instead, they are formed by our early environment starting with family dynamics. Then moving on to cultural narratives along with emotional experiences around wealth and scarcity. Over time, they become the lens through which we perceive the world and our place in it. This is the essence of wealth psychology as I understand it, which is tracing our external money patterns back to their internal roots.

When you notice yourself fearing money, avoiding it, obsessing over it, or feeling chronically "not enough," then there is always a deeper psychological blueprint driving that behavior or emotion. So how does this connect to the work of Jung, the legendary Swiss psychologist and founder of analytic psychology?

This is where it gets fascinating. Jung's work wasn't about surface-level behavior. It was about going beneath the conscious mind and into the realm of the unconscious. What is called the unconscious mind is where our deepest patterns and inherited stories live. If we want to truly understand why we relate to wealth the way we do instead of only changing a behavior, then we must go deeper and transform a belief.

We must explore the unconscious architecture of our financial lives. And that's where applying many of Jung's concepts come into play, particularly his concept about the collective unconscious. That becomes a powerful lens for understanding our wealth blueprint.

This is because we're not just influenced by personal experience, but we're also shaped by generational narratives. In addition to this, we are influenced deeply by archetypal energies as well as symbols of wealth and worth that have existed for centuries. The question is no longer, "Why do I do this with money?" but, rather, "What invisible system am I operating within, and how do I change it?"

The Hidden Code of Wealth

I have learned that our relationship with money isn't simply about earning or saving. It's about believing and becoming. Our financial reality is not merely the sum of our résumé, our background, or even our ambition. It is the result of an inner blueprint which is a deeply embedded script shaped by our early experiences. Other factors that shape our blueprint is cultural conditioning, and something even more mysterious and profound: the collective unconscious. All these aspects of ourselves—some visible, and some hidden—are a culmination of what I call the hidden codes of wealth.

So what, exactly, is the code of wealth? It is the unseen programming that governs our relationship to abundance, prosperity, and how we view success. It is not a formula but, rather, a psycho-emotional architecture of beliefs, inherited attitudes, and unconscious loyalties that influence our ability to receive or grow wealth.

Everyone has a code of wealth "blueprint" that serves as a template for how their money flows consistently as well as how they manage it. In addition, this blueprint also contains all of the inherited beliefs and experiences one has had with the concept of wealth or money itself by way of what Jung calls the collective unconscious.

Jung believed that beneath our personal unconscious lies a much deeper layer of psyche that he called the collective unconscious. Unlike individual memories or personal trauma, the collective unconscious is a universal inheritance, shared by all human beings.

It is composed of archetypes: symbolic energies, recurring motifs or storylines that have shaped human behavior for millennia. These archetypes aren't just myths. They are living patterns that operate in our lives, often without our realizing it. They show up in our dreams, in the roles we play, and yes, in the way we approach wealth.

Jung believed that these archetypes are not chosen but, instead, they are inherited. We are born into them. And unless we bring them into the light of consciousness, they dictate our behavior from the shadows.

Later scholars built on Jung's work and identified twelve primary archetypes: the Innocent, the Orphan, the Hero, the Caregiver, the Explorer, the Rebel, the Lover, the Creator, the Jester, the Sage, the Magician, and the Ruler. While all of these archetypes may live within us in varying degrees, only a few tend to dominate our relationship with money, in my opinion: the Orphan, the Martyr, the Ruler, and the Magician. Let's explore the four most relevant to wealth psychology:

The Orphan often feels abandoned by life and as of they've been left to fend for themselves. They carry a deep-seated belief that the world is unsafe, that help isn't coming, and that survival is always just barely achievable. Financially, the Orphan may avoid risks out of a subconscious loyalty to struggle.

By contrast, the Martyr is a shadow aspect of the Caregiver. They believe that self-sacrifice is noble, and they often give to others at the expense of themselves. Martyrs may resist receiving, undercharge for their work, or feel guilty about having "too much."

The Ruler, on the other hand, is the sovereign of their financial kingdom. This archetype is structured and takes full responsibility for their wealth. The Ruler doesn't merely earn, but they also build. They plan for legacy. They understand systems. They think in decades, not just paychecks.

The Magician is the alchemist. This archetype transforms inner awareness into outer abundance. The Magician doesn't hustle; they align. They use intuition and vision to manifest opportunities. Wealth, for them, flows when they are in sync with their deeper purpose.

It is important to note that these archetypes are not personality types. They are energetic modes or embodiments we move through, often without realizing it. Sometimes, we shift between them. Other times, one dominates our inner landscape for years, according to Jung.

The code of wealth or your blueprint is activated based on which archetypes hold power in your subconscious. You may consciously desire wealth, but if your subconscious is loyal to the Orphan's belief in struggle or the Martyr's belief in sacrifice, you will find yourself unconsciously pushing money away or chronically plateauing.

But, when you begin to identify which archetype is running your internal show, you can shift it. You can reclaim the Ruler within or can awaken the Magician. You can rewrite the emotional mythology that's shaping your finances and unlock the abundance that's been waiting beneath the surface all along. Jung believed that the most transformative journey a person could take was inward. According to Jung, the unconscious mind isn't just a shadowy place where memories are buried; it's a living realm filled with symbols, patterns, and archetypes.

One of the greatest tools in unlocking this realm is self-reflection. Your outer life reflects your inner world, and the patterns that repeat, especially around money are not random. They are revealing and are an invitation to look closer. So, how do you begin to uncover your wealth archetype? Start by turning inward. Jung believed that the psyche speaks through symbols, and these symbols often show up in our dreams, our habits, and our emotional responses—especially the ones that feel disproportionate to the moment. Begin to track your relationship with money in your daily life. Track not just the numbers but also the emotional waves that come with them.

Start asking yourself deeper, more probing questions: Do I feel uncomfortable receiving money or praise? Do I believe I must struggle to earn what I have? When I get close to financial success, do I unconsciously pull back, get overwhelmed, or lose momentum? Do I associate having money with freedom or with fear and isolation?

These questions are not meant to be answered in one sitting. They are windows into the unconscious. Pay attention to what rises to the surface, especially the discomfort. The mind has an incredible way of concealing what feels unsafe or unfamiliar. But the moment you bring awareness to your inner dialogue, you begin what Jung called the process of individuation which is the lifelong journey of becoming who you truly are by integrating unconscious material into conscious awareness.

As you reflect, also examine the money stories that shaped your early worldview. What did you hear growing up about money, success, or people who had "too much"? Was money spoken about openly, or was it taboo? Did you witness someone you love sacrifice endlessly and glorify struggle? Was scarcity the dominant narrative in your home? Were you taught to play it safe or to dream big?

These inherited stories don't just live in your memory. They live in your nervous system. They influence your financial decisions, even when you think you're being logical. This is where the archetypes begin to reveal themselves. For example, if you constantly overextend yourself for others but feel guilty about receiving, you may be unconsciously living out the Martyr archetype. If you avoid managing your finances because you believe you're "bad with money," you may be embodying the Orphan. If you quietly believe you're meant to do big things but keep waiting for permission or validation, the Ruler in you may be ready to emerge.

Jung never viewed these as good or bad, but as forces to be integrated. Once you name your dominant archetype, you reclaim your power. You are no longer acting from compulsion; you are choosing from awareness. But this isn't about boxing yourself into a category. You are not "just" the Martyr or "just" the Orphan.

Jung was clear: archetypes are not static roles. As mentioned, these archetypes are energetic patterns we move through. They are symbolic lenses, and they evolve as we evolve. You might begin your journey in the shadow of the Orphan but grow into the sovereignty of the Ruler or the insight of the Magician.

This is the beauty of individuation. It is not about becoming something else. It's about reclaiming the parts of yourself that were hidden, silenced, or distorted. This is why discovering your wealth archetype is so important. It's not about fixing yourself. It's about realizing that wealth doesn't start in your bank account. It starts in your subconscious. The more you understand your inner world, the more conscious your external results become. So, pay attention to the recurring themes in your financial life—not with judgment but with curiosity. Watch your reactions and listen to your stories. Question the beliefs you inherited and the behaviors they birthed.

Your archetype will reveal itself not with a label, but with a pattern. Once you see the pattern, you can begin to change it. You can interrupt the cycle. Then activate a new archetype—one that doesn't operate from fear or survival, but from vision, clarity, and alignment. Because at the heart of true wealth lies not just money but also consciousness. Once you have identified your dominant archetype, the real work begins. It involves not rejecting your dominant archetype but in integrating its shadow and unlocking its potential.

Jung emphasized that true transformation doesn't come from denying parts of us, but by bringing the unconscious into conscious awareness. The goal is not to escape the archetype but to evolve within it and to harness its gifts while healing its wounds.

The Orphan archetype must learn that safety and support are not fantasies. They often carry the unspoken belief that the world is fundamentally unsafe and that self-reliance is the only path to survival. But as the Orphan begins to heal, they realize that connection does not equal vulnerability, and that receiving help is not weakness, but it is wisdom. Trust is their turning point. When integrated, the Orphan becomes incredibly grounded. They possess an emotional strength forged through experience, and once they no longer identify with victimhood, they begin to build real wealth through clarity and resourcefulness.

The Martyr archetype must confront the story that their worth is measured by sacrifice. They often believe that if they are not giving everything away, inclusive of time, energy, and money, they are somehow less valuable. But this archetype must learn that it's not selfish to have boundaries. Healing begins when the Martyr understands that abundance for the self fuel's generosity for others. When transformed, the Martyr becomes the deeply nurturing Healer who is no longer depleted. They can serve without losing themselves, and wealth flows naturally when they allow reciprocity to enter their lives.

The Ruler archetype carries immense power, but that power must be anchored in emotional maturity. In its unbalanced state, the Ruler can become controlling or obsessed with status. But when integrated, the Ruler becomes a visionary leader. They know how to steward wealth not just for personal gain but also for legacy. A balanced ruler doesn't hoard control, but they create systems that empower others. Their mindset is one of long-term strategy and impact. This is the archetype that transforms businesses and even communities through conscious leadership in addition to financial acumen.

The Magician archetype is the bridge between the inner world and the outer result. They know that thought becomes form and that emotion creates momentum, but they must also learn the value of structure. Without grounding, the Magician can become lost in the habit of inconstant action. But when balanced, this archetype becomes an alchemist of opportunity. They bring visions to life with grace, guided by alignment rather than by force. The mature Magician understands that manifestation isn't magic. It's clarity, intention, and consistency paired with intuitive flow. They don't chase wealth. They attract it, because they've learned to trust their inner compass.

The Path Forward: Your Individuation Journey

So, what happens after this discovery? What happens after an archetype related to the archetypal wealth is named? This is when the hidden code starts to reveal itself. This is the moment where insight must become integration and where self-awareness evolves into self-leadership. This is not the end of the journey. It's the beginning of something far more powerful: transformation through conscious choice. It is where your wealth evolution shifts from knowledge to embodiment. It's no longer about learning who you are. It becomes living who you are.

It is how the individuation journey begins. Jung described individuation as the process of becoming your whole, authentic self which is basically the true self that exists beneath the masks, roles, traumas, and cultural expectations you've unconsciously carried.

This is not self-improvement. It's self-return—a remembering or a revealing of a homecoming to your inner truth. Jung taught that the psyche seeks wholeness. We are not meant to suppress our shadows or deny our complexity but, rather, to bring into dialogue all parts of ourselves including light and dark, strong and tender, and conscious and unconscious.

In the context of wealth, this means that becoming financially empowered isn't about copying someone else's strategy. It's about aligning your inner world so that prosperity can grow from the inside out. Most people are conditioned to chase wealth externally. This means more hours or more hustle. They miss the fact that true wealth arises from inner coherence. It grows in the soil of clarity and above all alignment.

This is why individuation is not just a psychological process as I understand it. It is a deeply practical one. As you begin to reclaim parts of yourself once buried or rejected, your entire energetic posture toward money begins to shift. You stop reacting and you start creating. Individuation is about returning to who you truly are. It's the process of peeling away the layers that were built from fear or societal expectations so that you can step into the truth of your identity. This is where agency is reclaimed. It's where vision becomes clear and sovereignty begins.

When you individuate, you stop living on autopilot and begin living with intention. Life no longer happens to you; it starts to flow from you. And this shift is exactly where success patterns begin to emerge. To be clear, these aren't borrowed habits or one-size-fits-all routines. They are natural outcomes of inner alignment that are custom expressions of your authentic self. If your code of wealth is the internal blueprint that silently shaped your past beliefs and behaviors around money, then success patterns are the conscious pathways you begin creating as you move forward. They are new choices made from awareness. They reflect the healed, integrated parts of you rather than the wounded parts.

These patterns aren't just external behaviors; they are lived experiences. They're embodied rather than performative, and they are deeply personal. The moment you name your archetype, something powerful happens. You bring unconscious patterns into conscious awareness. The fears or self-sabotage that once ran in the background start to lose their grip.

What was once an automatic response now becomes visible. And, once it's visible, you have something priceless: choice. In that space of choice, you discover your power. You begin to shift by alignment instead of by force. And, as your inner world transforms, your outer experience of wealth begins to reflect it. Why? Because, ultimately, wealth isn't just about money. It's a mirror that is showing you who you believe you are, what you feel you deserve, and how courageously you are willing to live in alignment with your truth.

What Change Begins To Look Like

Once you identify with an archetype, something subtle but powerful begins to shift. That change isn't necessarily dramatic. It's in the quiet, everyday moments where your relationship with money and self-worth gets activated. At first, this awareness can feel disorienting. You may notice discomfort rising in situations you used to move through on autopilot. But these moments aren't setbacks. They're signals. These are the earliest signs of awakening to changing your relationship with money.

Here are some questions that you may want to consider as you begin your journey of self-discovery:

- **Why do I hesitate to open my bank statements?**
Is it because I fear what I'll see? Or because some part of me believes I'm not capable of managing what's there?

- **Why do I feel unworthy when money flows in?**
Does receiving feel unsafe? Is there a hidden belief that says abundance must always be earned through struggle?

- **Why do I undercharge—or feel guilt when I ask for what I truly deserve?** Do I equate value with sacrifice? Was I taught that asking for more is greedy or ungrateful?

- **Why do I panic when I reach a new level of success?**
Is there a fear that it won't last? Or that I'll lose love, safety, or connection if I rise too high?

- **Why do I feel guilt when I prioritize my needs over others?** Was I conditioned to believe that worthiness comes from giving, not from being?

Your answers don't reflect random habits. They reveal patterns of your dominant wealth archetype that are still influencing your behavior from the unconscious. Each of these questions is a breadcrumb, leading you back to a deeper truth. They show you where your code is still running on outdated programming, asking to be seen, questioned, and rewritten.

This is what the process of individuation looks like in real life. As I've come to understand through my study of Jung's work, individuation isn't a dramatic overnight transformation. It's a daily practice of self-recognition. It's the slow, steady unfolding of your most authentic self as you bring the unconscious into the light of awareness.

Eventually, you begin to notice where you used to react. You learn to pause to observe your inner dialogue and question its source. You then feel the emotional charge around money, success, or self-worth. Rather than collapse into old behaviors, you stay present with it.

This is the power of consciousness. You move from being ruled by your archetype to partnering with it. You're no longer at the mercy of old patterns. Instead, you're in conversation with them.

You're interpreting the messages rather than being consumed by the noise.

Here's the beauty of this phase. The shifts may seem small, but they're foundational. Each moment of conscious choice becomes a vote for your future self. You're no longer looping the same wealth story. You're editing it. You're reclaiming authorship over your inner script. This is how healing begins: with awareness instead of a bang, and with presence rather than force. You develop a partnership with yourself and your evolving identity.

True change doesn't just show up in your bank account. It shows up in how you see yourself and treat yourself. It manifests itself in how you allow yourself to receive. How you allow yourself to expand and to take up space in the world. And that, right there, is the beginning of wealth embodiment.

Once you begin to engage with the archetype you most identify with consciously, a quiet but profound transformation begins. You're no longer trapped in cycles of self-judgment or striving to fix what's wrong with you. Instead, you start to recognize that what once felt like a flaw was actually a form of protection your psyche adopted to survive and to stay safe.

This is where the reclamation begins. Individuation is not about cutting off or rejecting the parts of yourself shaped by your archetype. It's about bringing them into awareness, learning their language, and guiding them into alignment. These parts aren't problems to be solved. Instead, they are raw material for your becoming. Let's explore how each archetype transforms when met with presence, compassion, and conscious partnership

The Orphan

The Orphan archetype is originally shaped by early experiences of abandonment, betrayal, neglect, or unreliable support. Somewhere along the way, the Orphan internalizes a core belief: "If I don't protect myself, no one else will."

In response, they cultivate fierce independence, becoming self-reliant out of necessity, not choice. They are often skeptical of help and deeply cautious about demonstrating vulnerability.

Their resilience becomes a form of armor or an impressive strength on the outside, but one that can also wall them off from receiving the very connection and support they deeply crave. Beneath the surface, there is often a profound yearning, a longing to feel safe, to trust, and to belong. Yet the fear of being hurt keeps the Orphan locked in a cycle of doing everything alone, sometimes even unconsciously pushing away the support they desire.

Through the process of individuation, the Orphan begins to experience a softening. They come to realize that vulnerability is not weakness. It's a bridge to connection, authentic support, and a life where they don't have to carry the entire weight alone.

Little by little, the Orphan practices new, courageous behaviors such as asking for help without attaching shame to it; receiving care without suspicion or guilt; And allowing themselves to be held emotionally or even financially at times.

They discover that true strength is not rigid self-reliance but, rather, flexible interdependence. It's the ability to both give and receive support, and to both stand strong and allow others to stand with you.

Through this integration, the Orphan evolves into a grounded, resourceful creator who draws strength not just from within but also from the connections they nurture. They no longer walk alone. They lead with both sovereignty and community, knowing that true independence includes the courage to lean when needed, and the strength to allow collaboration and above all trust to be part of their foundation.

The Martyr

The Martyr archetype is shaped by a deeply ingrained belief that love and worth must be earned through sacrifice. They become expert givers or supporters ready to meet the needs of others, often at the expense of their own. For the Martyr, prioritizing themselves can feel uncomfortable, selfish, or even dangerous. Their generosity is genuine, but it's often entwined with subtle threads of guilt balled up into fear that, if they stop giving, they'll lose connection or love. Over time, this pattern can lead to chronic depletion and most often an identity built around being needed rather than being truly seen.

Individuation invites the Martyr to rewrite this story. It challenges them to see that self-honoring is stewardship, not selfishness. It's stewardship of their own energy. The first signs of transformation are often small but radical. They include raising their rates in business and believing they are worth it; saying "no" without a long explanation or apology; resting without guilt; and allowing themselves to receive as much as they give.

They begin to understand that their energy is very sacred. When they care for themselves, they actually have more love and more presence to offer the world. Through this reclamation, the Martyr evolves into someone who gives from overflow rather than obligation, who nurtures others without abandoning themselves, and who understands that their value is intrinsic.

Their generosity becomes magnetic and rooted in true self-worth rather than martyrdom. Through the process of individuation, they create a life where service to others coexists with deep service to themselves and a life where they are no longer erased by their giving but expanded by it.

The Ruler

The Ruler archetype is often characterized by a natural drive for leadership as well authority. At their best, they have the capacity to be powerfully effective with organizing, protecting, and guiding with steady vision. However, when the Ruler operates from an unconscious or unintegrated place, their gift of leadership can become entangled with scarcity. Many will also fiercely chase the relentless pursuit of external validation. Driven by a deep need to control outcomes through achievement, the Ruler may indeed build successful businesses, have growing wealth or have prestigious titles. But, underneath the surface, they may feel emotionally disconnected. This disconnect is often associated with the overwhelming pressure to maintain and even defend what they have built. Without realizing it, the Ruler can begin to chase outcomes as a way to soothe deeper insecurities or to validate their existence. This constant striving can leave them feeling isolated even at the height of their achievements.

Individuation invites the Ruler to turn inward. It challenges them to step off the treadmill of endless ambition and ask the deeper questions such as: What am I truly building? For whom am I building it? Why does it matter?

As the Ruler turns from ego to essence, and from domination to contribution, a profound transformation occurs. They realize that true power comes from conscious stewardship rather than from control.

At that point, leadership is no longer about maintaining an empire. It becomes about serving something greater than themselves. The Ruler begins to reorient their ambition toward purpose. They become less concerned with how much they own and more focused on what they are cultivating for others. They build systems that are not extractive but generative systems that uplift.

Through this evolution, the Ruler becomes a visionary leader. This leadership uses power consciously and compassionately. They create structures that endure beyond their personal influence. These legacies benefit not just themselves but also entire communities, industries, and future generations. They measure success not merely by numbers or titles, but by the quality of impact. Success is also measured by how many lives are improved, and by the values embedded in everything they create.

Their leadership becomes catalytic, meaning it sparks and multiplies the success of others. They become architects of possibility, not just gatekeepers of wealth.

The Magician

The Magician is naturally gifted with intuition and vison. They often have an almost otherworldly ability to sense possibilities others can't yet see. Ideas come easily to them, as do flashes of insight and creative inspiration. They are innovators and impactful visionaries at heart.

However, when this archetype is unintegrated, their energy can become scattered. They may find themselves constantly chasing new ideas, starting many projects but completing few. Their focus drifts easily, pulled by the next exciting possibility before the last one has had time to mature. In this state, their immense creative potential remains locked in the realm of imagination. Their dreams stay dreams, never fully realized in the physical world. The ungrounded Magician often struggles with frustration, feeling like they are overflowing with potential but unable to turn their visions into tangible, lasting results. They might feel misunderstood when reality doesn't move as fast as their mind.

But this is not a flaw. It is simply a call for integration. As the Magician matures through the individuation journey, they begin to understand that inspiration alone is not enough. They realize that vision must be paired with form, and that intuition must be anchored by action. This is where true magic begins.

The evolving Magician learns to ground the mystical with the practical. Discipline is embraced as a sacred container for their gifts. They begin to trust in timelines, in incremental progress, and in the unseen momentum that builds through sustained effort.

For the Magician, the realization that structure and being consistent are not enemies of creativity. Instead, they are the scaffolding that allow progress to take place. Through this process, the Magician transforms into a true creative alchemist. This means that they are no longer caught in endless cycles of inspiration without execution. They master the art of manifestation and turning raw ideas into real-world impact. Flow with follow-through are married and seen as progression which leads to implementation. Their work becomes a living expression of beauty, purpose, and precision.

The integrated Magician doesn't abandon their dreams. They realize that the act of creation is a dance between vision and reality, and between soul and structure. Through this transformation, the Magician becomes not just a dreamer, but also a builder of new worlds.

Closing Remarks:

If there's one profound truth to take from this chapter, let it be this: Wealth is not random, and it is never just material. It follows invisible patterns and what I have come to call the hidden codes of wealth. These codes are etched deep into the psyche, beneath the surface of logic or conscious thought. They quietly shape how we relate to money in all facets, even sabotage.

Until these psychological patterns are brought to light, we remain at their mercy, repeating inherited financial scripts that keep us confined to survival. What I discovered through years of inquiry is that true wealth doesn't begin in the outer world. It doesn't start with promotions or business strategies. It begins within. It begins in the architecture of the mind, and in the beliefs and emotional imprints we absorbed long before we ever opened a bank account. This realization is what led me to leave behind the predictable paths of personal finance and enter the far more revealing terrain of depth psychology.

Jung understood that much of human behavior is not driven by what we know, but by what we have not yet made conscious. The archetypes Jung described aren't just mythic symbols. They're psychological blueprints that influence how we approach success, how we experience failure, and how we hold or reject wealth.

Once you begin to work with these archetypes, and once you identify your dominant success pattern, you no longer feel like you're pushing a boulder uphill. You tap into a different rhythm altogether. You gain access to the inner architecture of wealth or the part of you that already knows how to generate and hold abundance.

These hidden codes are not permanent imprints. They are malleable, and they can be reprogrammed. When that shift occurs, everything changes. Wealth stops being something you chase. Instead, it becomes something that flows to you. That's the real secret: alignment. When your values, your beliefs, and your inner archetypes are integrated, wealth arrives not as a fluke, but as a natural consequence. It's about becoming so aligned with your true self that money becomes a mirror of your wholeness instead of your worth. It is the energetic signature of an integrated life.

CHAPTER TWO

Synchronicity And Wealth: Is It Really Just Coincidence?

"Synchronicity is the coming together of inner and outer events in a way that cannot be explained by cause and effect and that is meaningful to the observer."

—*Carl Jung*

When we speak of Coincidence, we speak of those uncanny moments when an inner impulse or a sudden insight appears to be answered in the outer world by an event so perfectly timed that it defies any ordinary explanation. You might be wrestling with a big decision, and then you glance up to see a billboard offering exactly the phrase you needed to hear. You could be wrestling with self-doubt about your next creative step, only to stumble across an invitation or connection that seems tailor-made to usher you forward. This is the experience Jung described as synchronicity, an acausal connecting principle he explored most fully in his 1952 essay, "Synchronicity: An Acausal Connecting Principle," collected in The Interpretation of Nature and the Psyche. In Jung's view, these synchronistic events are not anomalies or happenstance; they are brief windows into the deeper architecture of reality or moments when the invisible currents of our unconscious are reflected in the tangible world, as though the cosmos itself were echoing our inner state.

For those of us investigating the psychology of wealth, synchronicity can feel like a secret corridor opening at precisely the point of our greatest need. If Chapter One revealed the hidden codes of wealth, then Chapter Two invites you to peer behind another curtain. Here, we witness the dynamic interplay between inner alignment and outer opportunity, where meaningful coincidences become signposts guiding you toward deeper levels of abundance.

Jung famously observed, "When an inner situation is not made conscious, it appears outside as fate." In other words, the conflicts we ignore within ourselves have a way of manifesting as events that we often dismiss as random chance. Yet those events are anything but random. They are the psyche's way of speaking through circumstance, calling our attention to the places where our inner and outer worlds are out of harmony.

Imagine you have been quietly incubating an entrepreneurial idea but lack the confidence to act. Then, almost overnight, you find yourself seated next to a successful founder at a community gathering. The conversation flows, the founder offers a key referral, and suddenly your project has momentum.

Or perhaps you have been wrestling with feelings of scarcity, only to receive a gift and an unexpected scholarship that seems to land at precisely the moment doubt threatened to derail you. These are not mere coincidences; they are vivid reminders that psyche and matter can dance together, beyond linear cause and effect. Recognizing and interpreting the messages held in these meaningful coincidences is essential for anyone seeking to align their internal world with the flow of external resources and wealth.

Synchronicity asks us to listen as well as pay attention not only to our plans and strategies but also to the subtle whispers of the universe that occur when our outer reality mirrors our inner transformation. By cultivating this awareness, we learn to move in tandem with the deeper rhythms of life, allowing serendipitous opportunities to guide us toward our most authentic expression of abundance.

Jung insisted that the gateway to synchronistic insight lies in increasing consciousness: deliberately tuning into your dreams, honoring your intuitions, and attending to the emotional undercurrents that flow beneath your ordinary thoughts. With this mindset in place, we can recognize the uncanny "right place, right time" moments that propel us forward.

Although we cannot peer into anyone's private psyche, we can observe how public figures embody the very principles of synchronicity in their rise to lasting prosperity. In my research into the past, I found three case studies to illuminate how individuals from vastly different backgrounds tapped into meaningful coincidences and inner alignment to build extraordinary wealth from scratch.

Case Study:
Oprah Winfrey's Synchronicity in Action

Oprah Winfrey's ascent from regional talk-show host to global media icon offers a vivid illustration of how financial synchronicities can gather momentum and crystallize into enduring prosperity. In 1986, when A.M. Chicago teetered on the edge of cancellation, no market analysis could have

SYNCHRONICITY AND WEALTH · 45

predicted its transformation into the Oprah Winfrey Show, nor the seismic success that would follow. Yet, at each critical juncture, Oprah encountered what can only be called synchronistic support.

One morning, confidant and early executive producer Bill Geddie happened to mention an editorial shift that resonated precisely with Oprah's unspoken sense of the show's heart. So, she pivoted on the air to share her own story of personal struggle.

Within days, a viewer's heartfelt letter poured in, affirming that the authenticity of her confession was exactly what the audience craved. Then, when ratings plateaued, an unexplained opening in the coveted 4:00 p.m. slot appeared, propelling the show into prime afternoon viewership and transforming Oprah from a regional curiosity into a national phenomenon.

Viewed through the lens of synchronicity, these moments were far more than random luck or the byproduct of conventional networking. Each event arrived when Oprah's inner world was wrestling with the yearnings she carried for genuine connection. The external world, in response, offered milestones that validated and amplified her emerging vision.

Rather than forcing a new format or chasing demographic data, Oprah honored these invitations. She embraced the unexpected phone call, the timely letter, and the slot change with the same openness she brought to her own inner process. In doing so, she demonstrated how honoring synchronistic prompts and those uncanny alignments between psyche and circumstance can catalyze a compounding effect. One breakthrough builds upon another, weaving together the strands of opportunity into a tapestry of lasting wealth.

Case Study:
Howard Schultz's Milan Epiphany and the Birth of Starbucks' Global Empire

Long before Starbucks became synonymous with the global coffeehouse experience, Howard Schultz was simply the director of marketing for a small Seattle-based coffee bean retailer. In 1983, on a business trip to Milan to report on espresso machines for his company's newsletter, Schultz found himself wandering into Italian cafés so alive with warmth that he felt he had stumbled into another world.

More than the rich aroma of roasted beans, he encountered a vibrant gathering place where people lingered over multiple cups, forging community in a way that no American coffee shop had yet mastered. There was no business plan behind this immersion, only the magnetic pull of an idea whose time had come.

Schultz later reflected that he had gone to Milan to write copy about equipment yet left the city with a profound vision: "I knew immediately that Starbucks needed to reimagine itself as more than a retailer of coffee equipment and beans. It needed to become a place."

That instantaneous insight was a synchronistic spark. It felt like an answer to a deeper question he had not consciously asked: What if coffee could be the catalyst for genuine human connection and belonging?

When Schultz returned to Seattle and shared his vision, the company's founders resisted. They were focused on the wholesale coffee-business model Schultz had inherited, and they worried that transforming their stores into full-fledged cafés would dilute their brand.

Yet Schultz could not ignore the synchronicity of his experience. He sensed that the universe had marked this revelation with uncanny timing. A single overseas trip, a handful of café visits and, suddenly, a new archetypal role beckoned the visionary leader who brings people together.

Rather than abandon his insight, Schultz followed it. He left Starbucks to launch his own chain, Il Giornale, funded by a local investor who happened to be a family friend and provided yet another synchronistic opening.

Il Giornale's early success validated Schultz's hunch. Within two years, he returned to purchase Starbucks itself, merging his fledgling cafés with the original stores. The acquisition was locked in on Valentine's Day of 1987, as coffee culture was poised to boom, and it felt less like a negotiated takeover and more like destiny aligning the outer world with Schultz's inner calling.

Under Schultz's leadership, Starbucks expanded rapidly. Each new store opening was often accompanied by its own synchronistic signature: a prime retail location became unexpectedly available, an influential community leader endorsed the concept, or a regional distributor reached out unprompted. Schultz himself has acknowledged that these moments of serendipity were not the result of forceful strategy alone but emerged when he trusted his inner vision enough to act courageously.

Today, Starbucks operates in over eighty countries, and its global valuation measured in the tens of billions. But the true lesson of Howard Schultz's journey is not the scale of his empire. It lies in how financial synchronicities can compound when an individual honors the secret invitations that life offers.

Schultz's Milan epiphany was the first in a series of coordinated events that, taken together, illustrate how inner alignment can magnetize extraordinary opportunities. By examining Schultz's path from marketing director to the architect of a cultural phenomenon, we see how synchronicity and success patterns intertwine. A chance assignment to Milan became a transformative vision; a hesitant presentation to company founders became a strategic spin-off; and the purchase of Starbucks became the launchpad for a global movement.

These were not random strokes of luck. They were the unfolding of a deeper intelligence responding to Schultz's readiness to innovate. In honoring each synchronistic prompt and by pitching the café concept despite skepticism, by securing serendipitous investment, and by expanding precisely when the market was ripe; Schultz demonstrated how wealth follows the hidden codes of inner conviction meeting outer possibility.

Case Study:
Sara Blakely's Serendipitous Path to Spanx

Long before Sara Blakely became a self-made billionaire, she was a frustrated young salesperson with a simple yet revolutionary idea: footless pantyhose. One summer evening in 1998, Blakely was preparing for a party. Irritated by the bulky seams of her pantyhose under white pants, she grabbed a pair of scissors and cut off the feet. In that impulsive moment, born of everyday discomfort, she felt a spark. It was the first whisper of what would become Spanx.

That spark, however, needed more than determination. It needed the universe to conspire. Over the next months, Blakely devoted her evenings to prototyping and convinced herself she could build a business, despite having no background in fashion or manufacturing.

She invested her entire savings into developing a basic prototype. Then came the first synchronistic surprise. Blakely cold-called hosiery mills nationwide seeking a manufacturer, and all but one refused. The mill owner's receptionist happened to be the only female engineer in the company, and when she heard Blakely's pitch, she immediately connected her to her boss. That introduction was not on the mill's typical agenda, yet it felt the right door opening at exactly the right time.

The second synchronistic twist arrived a week before her first major sales meeting. Blakely had secured an appointment with a Neiman Marcus buyer, but she hadn't yet printed samples or even formed a clear presentation. While boarding a flight to Dallas, she struck up a conversation with the man in the next seat who was an executive from a department store chain. She shared her vision offhandedly, and he encouraged her to refine her pitch. He offered to introduce her to contacts in retail.

Back on the ground, that same executive made an unexpected call, connecting Blakely directly with the very Neiman Marcus buyer she was about to see. Blakely walked into that meeting with two gifts: her passionate prototype and the unspoken assurance that she wasn't alone. When she demonstrated Spanx to the Neiman Marcus buyer who happened to be a friend of the mill owner's engineer, the buyer was so intrigued that she placed an immediate order.

Blakely later learned that this buyer had once taken a personal risk on a fledgling designer and trusted her intuition enough to do so again. That trust, too, felt like synchronicity: a meta-pattern of alignment among three women who all showed up for Blakely's idea at pivotal moments.

From there, Spanx's ascent felt propelled by a stream of timely events: a glowing feature on a popular morning show, impromptu celebrity endorsements from the red carpet, and an Oprah "Favorite Thing" selection in 2000 that sent orders skyrocketing overnight.

Each of these milestones arrived not because Blakely meticulously calculated them, but because she had laid the groundwork of inner alignment in believing in her idea without guarantee of success and remained open to the uncanny openings that followed. Looking back, Blakely describes these moments as more than lucky breaks. They were "God winks," as she calls them, or synchronistic affirmations that she was on the right path.

Her willingness to heed each prompt, and to pursue opportunities even when logic suggested caution, allowed those coincidences to compound into an empire now valued at over a billion dollars. Sara Blakely's journey shows us that synchronicity in wealth creation is not a matter of biblical fortune but of co-creative readiness.

By nurturing our inner vision, trusting our intuitive sparks, and leaning into the unplanned connections that arise, we transform chance encounters into catalytic career milestones. When we honor those moments, we discover that prosperity often unfolds not through rigid strategy alone, but rather through the dynamic interplay of our deepest convictions and the world's mysterious encouragement.

To train yourself in the art of cultivating synchronicity, start by softening the speed of your life. In the spaces between tasks or while you linger over your coffee, notice when something out of the ordinary occurs. Perhaps you run into someone you desperately needed to meet, receive an unexpected email that feels perfectly timed, or dream a vivid scene that seems to answer a question you have not yet asked aloud.

Resist the urge to shrug these moments off as mere chance. Instead, allow yourself to wonder: What is this pointing me toward? Next, anchor your awareness through writing. Keep a dedicated journal not only for your financial plans and to-do lists, but also for synchronicity entries and the inner state you were carrying at that moment.

Perhaps you note how a late-night thought about launching a side business was met the next morning with an invitation to collaborate, or how a recurring dream about architecture coincided with discovering an investment opportunity in real estate you hadn't considered.

Over weeks and months, you'll begin to trace the threads: certain questions you hold, certain emotional tensions, and the ways the universe answers in kind. Beyond noticing and recording, there is a third subtle practice to include. That is setting clear intentions without grasping for control.

Jung cautioned against treating synchronicity like a magic trick or forcing the world to comply with your desires. Instead, hold your financial goals with clarity and know the outcome you wish to manifest. Stay open to the myriad roads the psyche may conjure to get you there. This is not wishful thinking. It is a co-creative partnership where you provide the vision, and synchronicity provides the surprises that carry that vision into reality.

When you weave these three practices together, you begin to transform from a market-driven strategist into a participant in an unfolding dialogue between your inner world and the outer one. Opportunities cease to feel like flukes and start to feel like echoes of your own emerging purpose. Doors that were once hidden spring because you have become attuned to the deeper currents that guide them. In this way, synchronicity becomes a foundational pillar of your wealth psychology rather than a curiosity or a gimmick.

It reminds you that true abundance is an inside-out phenomenon. By aligning your consciousness with your highest aims, you magnetize the resources that make sustained prosperity possible. As you continue, you may grow even more sensitive to these invitations. Your journey toward wealth may become a richly supported odyssey guided by the invisible intelligence that moves through us all rather than a solo expedition of hard work.

Once you have noticed and journaled these meaningful coincidences, you'll start seeing patterns that trace back to the core archetypes we explored in Chapter One. Let's now explore how synchronicity can serve as an archetypal corrective, guiding each inner pattern toward greater wholeness.

The Archetypal Roots of Financial Coincidences

Recall the four archetypes that served as our compass in Chapter One: the Orphan, the Martyr, the Ruler, and the Magician. Each carries its own blueprint of trust, power, sacrifice, and vision. As you continue to excavate these patterns within yourself, you may notice that synchronicity arrives precisely when one archetype is out of balance, almost as if the universe itself steps in to offer a course correction.

When the Orphan's wound of isolation has led you to believe you must always go it alone, a chance meeting with a mentor, or perhaps a new acquaintance at a workshop you almost skipped, can arrive like a beacon of support you didn't even know you desperately needed. That encounter may feel so perfectly timed that it defies rational explanation, reminding you that trust is more than possible. It is essential to your journey.

Likewise, when the Martyr archetype has you trapped in cycles of endless giving and emotional depletion, synchronicity can break through in the form of an unexpected gift or a surprise bonus. Even a kind word from a stranger can resonate like divine permission to receive. In that moment, you realize that generosity and self-care are not enemies but, rather, partners, and that abundance is not meant to be hoarded in silent sacrifice but to flow in a dance of giving and receiving.

When the Ruler's need for control hardens into rigidity, every decision feels like a high-stakes gamble, and you may find synchronicity materializing as an unforeseen challenge that shifts your perspective. Perhaps a sudden market shift forces you to innovate in ways you never imagined, or a disruption in your carefully mapped plans leads you to discover a purpose-driven project that ignites both passion and profit.

This abrupt detour can feel like a cosmic nudge, guiding you from the narrow confines of power used for its own sake into the expansive realm of leadership used in service of something greater than yourself.

And, for the Magician, whose boundless creativity can sometimes scatter into a thousand unfinished projects, synchronicity often arrives as a clarifying flash or an insight so vivid it compresses months of brainstorming into a single, actionable vision. You might be wrestling with whether to launch a new product or pivot an existing service and, suddenly, a conversation crystallizes all the loose threads into one coherent strategy.

In that instant, you understand that true magic isn't found in unbridled inspiration alone, but also in the alchemical fusion of imagination and disciplined follow-through. These synchronistic prompts are not random miracles bestowed upon the lucky. They are reflections of a psyche in motion and a consciousness that is beginning to realign with its deepest callings.

They emerge in the spaces where we have outgrown old patterns and taken the first steps toward integration. When you learn to recognize these meaningful coincidences, you discover that your inner journey and outer reality are two sides of the same unfolding story. In acknowledging these moments, you open yourself to a richer, more cocreative relationship with wealth, and one that honors both the unseen currents of the unconscious and the tangible rewards that flow when mind, heart, and circumstance move in harmony.

Science, Skepticism, and the Art of Meaning

Skeptics often dismiss synchronicity as little more than wishful thinking or an appealing narrative that lacks the rigor of reproducible causality. Yet Jung never sought to replace empirical science with mystical explanation. He proposed synchronicity as a complementary lens, enriching our understanding of human experience by honoring the significance we inherently seek in the world.

Contemporary neuroscience offers striking parallels. Research in pattern recognition shows that our brains are exquisitely tuned to detect order in apparent randomness which opens us to the meaningful coincidences we call synchronicity. Likewise, studies of the placebo effect reveal how our beliefs and expectations can trigger real physiological change, demonstrating that meaning itself can exert measurable influence on outcomes.

In the realm of finance, these insights carry profound implications. Traditional models treat markets as mechanistic systems governed solely by rational actors and data points, but behavioral economics has upended that view by showing how emotion and perception drive decisions just as powerfully as spreadsheets do. When a synchronistic event aligns perfectly with your inner conviction, it can unlock confidence you didn't know you had, spark creative problem-solving, and catalyze actions that reshape your trajectory.

In this way, synchronicity is a bridge connecting your inner sense of purpose to the tangible steps that bring it to life. Recognizing this doesn't require abandoning critical thinking. Rather, it calls for an expanded framework that includes both causality and meaningful coincidence as valid guides in our personal and financial evolution.

As you cultivate sensitivity to these synchronistic signals, your very conception of wealth begins to shift. Remarkably, you begin to notice that prosperity is no longer a static endpoint or a goal to be checked off. Instead, it becomes a living current that flows through adaptability and a deep inner clarity.

You discover that the most direct path to your objectives may be a winding journey marked by unexpected signposts instead of a rigid plan. This may look like a serendipitous introduction to an investor, a chance insight in a conversation, or a sudden flash of inspiration that can redirect you toward opportunities conventional strategy would never have unearthed.

Over time, you realize that your relationship to money and your sense of purpose are not separate tracks but intertwined narratives. Your financial decisions begin to reflect your deepest values rather than merely short-term gains. You learn to move in partnership with life's hidden currents therefore trusting that when you act from alignment, you will witness resources appearing and breakthroughs emerging in ways that reinforce your growth. In this new paradigm, prosperity is less a matter of accumulation and more a matter of resonance—a continuous dance between your evolving self and the abundant possibilities the world presents.

Aligned Action Attracts the Unseen

Synchronicity is not a fluke. I have learned it is a law that transcends linear logic yet governs the very architecture of success at the deepest level. So, if success seems far away, ask not only what you must do but also who you must become. What does "success" mean to your soul? What image does it carry? What feeling arises when you visualize it? Until you know what you are actually trying to align with, your efforts will be scattered.

Start to see the map that is being drawn just beneath your conscious plans, and take aligned action. Synchronicity is not an excuse for passivity. On the contrary, it demands your participation. But the action you take must be infused with clarity, not compulsion. Move when it feels true, not when it feels forced. Speak what you mean, not what you think others want. Invest where your soul feels stirred and go with that feeling unequivocally and steady.

These are the acts that carry vibrational weight. When synchronicity shows up, do not dismiss it as chance. Every synchronicity is a mirror of your own readiness. In this light, the universe is not simply a stage; it is a co-creator. Jung wrote, "It is not only possible but highly probable that psyche and matter are two different aspects of one and the same thing." That "thing" is reality itself, shaped as much by meaning as by matter. When you become aligned within, the world aligns around you. When you speak the truth of your being, the invisible moves to meet you.

The moment your inner world vibrates with the clarity of your true desire, the outer world will begin to echo back its answer. And when it does, don't just call it coincidence. Call it what it truly is: a response.

The Story of Daniel

Daniel was a mid-level executive in his late thirties, raised in a family that praised humility and distrusted wealth. His grandfather lost everything during a market crash and turned bitter toward ambition. His mother often said, "Money is the root of all evil" and celebrated frugality as moral superiority.

By all external accounts, Daniel was doing well. He earned a stable income, was respected in his field, and even had ideas for starting his own company. But each time he neared the edge of that expansion or when investors showed interest or collaborators came forward, there was always something that would go wrong. He would delay answering an important email, or he would second-guess his pitch.

At first, Daniel blamed circumstance. Then, with time and reflection, he realized the problem wasn't "out there." The problem was within. Daniel was afraid of success because of what was operating behind his beliefs systems mean: betrayal of his roots, abandonment of his family's values, and the risk of becoming "one of them." His conscious ambition clashed with unconscious loyalty to ancestral wounds.

Through therapy, Daniel was shown the unconscious programs running in the background. The shadow revealed itself through self-sabotage, missed calls, and procrastination. Self-doubt masked as family collective beliefs mixed in with his own definitions of success and wealth.

Instead of bypassing this inner conflict, Daniel engaged it. He began to dialogue with his resistance, journaling letters to his younger self and envisioning having imaginary dialogues with his grandfather who initially triggered the generational belief of scarcity and frugality. He eventually got to a place where he reframed his beliefs associated with wealth so that he could heal this generational scarcity.

Daniel kept his new beliefs about success and wealth consistent. This aligned his inner thoughts with his outer reality, resulting in the creation of synchronicities. His new consistent beliefs coupled with his burning desire to create a business manifested into chance meeting a mentor at an airport; a call from an investor he hadn't heard from in months; and a successful product launch with no major hurdles.

Daniel didn't have to force success, because he became congruent with it. He stopped trying to win and started becoming someone who could hold success without guilt. He was no longer just achieving. Instead, he was integrating. This is not a fable. This is point of view, and it is vibration with alignment.

Closing Remarks:

As Chapter Two draws to a close, I invite you to revisit your memory of meaningful coincidences. Look back on those striking moments when an inner question seemed to be answered by an outer event. These are invitations to step more fully into your power, to refine your purpose, and to expand your capacity for abundance. In Chapter Three, we will explore Success Patterns, the conscious, repeatable habits and mind-body practices that sustain these synchronistic currents over the long haul, transforming fleeting opportunities into lasting prosperity.

But, before we embark on that next phase, pause and honor the synchronistic moments you've already experienced. They are the universe's way of lighting your path forward, guiding you toward the wealth that awaits when mind, heart, and circumstance move in harmony.

CHAPTER THREE

The Success Archetype: Defining the Hidden Pattern

"One does not become enlightened by imagining figures of light, but by making the darkness conscious."

—*Carl G. Jung, Psychology and Alchemy (Collected Works, Vol. 12)*

Synchronicity reveals when opportunity arrives, and the success archetype shows us who we must become to step through the door it opens. In the same way that Jung mapped our inner world through archetypes, those primordial patterns etched into the collective unconscious, we can chart the personal blueprint that underlies lasting achievement.

This chapter guides you through the art and science of psychological profiling, not as a means of permanent labeling, but rather as a powerful tool of self-discovery. You will unearth the success archetype that resonates with your deepest strengths, values, and vision, learn how it weaves together with the hidden codes of wealth from Chapter One, and discover the practices that breathe your archetype into daily life.

Four Foundational Success Archetypes

In my research of entrepreneurs and leaders, four foundational success archetypes repeatedly emerged as the most potent engines of prosperity. Each archetype represents a unique constellation of psychological energies, gifts of personality and purpose that, when consciously embraced, ignite extraordinary achievement. Yet each also harbors a shadow side: unconscious impulses that, if left unexamined, can sabotage even the most brilliant efforts. These foundational success archetypes are the Visionary Leader, the Creative Alchemist, the Resilient Builder, and the Empowered Healer.

The visionary leader is defined by an uncanny ability to see new horizons long before others do. This archetype thrives on pioneering ideas mainly. Also know for setting bold directions and pushing towards galvanizing teams to pursue an ambitious future. Visionary leaders tend to be extremely magnetic, drawing supporters with their conviction and clarity of purpose. Their greatest strength lies in strategic foresight and piecing together emerging trends into a coherent roadmap that everyone can rally behind.

However, in the absence of conscious reflection, this very gift can tip into authoritarianism. The Visionary's clarity may become rigid. Their confidence may morph into dogmatism, and their inspiring guidance may move into an uncompromising direction. Teams can often feel stifled where voices are unheard and collaboration reduced to rote execution. True mastery for the Visionary leader lies in balancing the drive to innovate with an openness to dissent, treating feedback not as a threat but as a vital source of refinement, and wielding influence as an invitation rather than as an edict.

The Creative Alchemist inhabits the realm of pure possibility where raw imagination transmutes the ordinary into the extraordinary. This archetype is a conduit for innovation sparked by inspiration and fueled by intuition. This archetype is perpetually searching for the next revolutionary idea.

Creative Alchemists excel at bridging distant concepts. This includes rewiring conventional wisdom as well as painting vivid new paradigms on the canvas of possibility. Yet, without grounding discipline, their visions can fracture into distraction. Far too often they leap from one exciting concept to another, leaving half-built prototypes and abandoned dreamscapes in their wake.

The key for the Creative Alchemist is learning to temper boundless creativity with rigorous process. That means establishing clear detailed milestones while inviting honest critique. This also means cultivating daily routines that transform flashes of brilliance into tangible outcomes, all while preserving the very spark that ignites their genius.

The Resilient Builder is the architect of sustainable progress. Possessing deep wells of resourcefulness, this archetype weathers storms and nurtures steady growth. This archetype is also well with adaptability and communal orientation with others. Resilient builders excel at forging lasting alliances of which they excel at mobilizing networks and adapting plans in the face of adversity. It's like master sailors adjusting their sails to every unexpected gust. Their strength lies in constructing sturdy foundations like implementing effective processes within systems that endure market shifts and personal challenges alike.

Yet, when caution calcifies into rigidity, opportunity can slip through the cracks. Builders may cling to proven formulas or worse resist the very creativity and risk that fuels future expansion. The path forward for the Resilient Builder involves consciously inviting experimentation. That means treating small failures as data points. Learning to co–create innovations with stakeholders, and re-framing change not as a threat but as the lifeblood of renewal.

The Empowered Healer channels generosity, empathy, and service into a wellspring of abundance. This archetype knows that genuine wealth flows through upliftment, whether in guiding a mentee to new heights or structuring business models that return value to communities.

Their gift is creating loyal followings and fostering trust through authentic care. Yet, in its shadow form, the Empowered Healer's compassion can become self-erasure, dissolving boundaries to the point of depletion. Unchecked, their drive to give can erode personal reserves affecting the emotional bandwidth that can sometimes lead to physical depletion. This, ultimately causing a person to burn out or being resentful.

True empowerment for the Empowered Healer arises from embracing reciprocity. This means honoring personal limits continuously and understanding that self-care is an essential act of service. By learning to receive as well as to give, the Empowered Healer transforms generosity into a sustainable cycle of abundance that nourishes both giver and recipient. This is very profound with benefits for all parties involved.

In recognizing these four success archetypes and acknowledging their shadows, you gain a map for your own journey. You learn not only which archetype resonates most deeply with your strengths, but you also discover where hidden impulses may be quietly undermining your path. When illuminated by conscious practice, each archetype's gifts can shine without casting the long shadows of unexamined behaviors, empowering you to step fully into the pattern that unlocks your richest potential.

If you find yourself resonating strongly with one archetype, that is powerful—but most of us are far more complex. We are not confined to a single pattern of success. Instead, like colors blending on an artist's canvas, the archetypes merge and evolve within us, creating a living, multidimensional portrait of our strengths, challenges, and potential. Together, they shape not just who we are, but who we are continually becoming.

Imagine someone whose big-picture vision and strategic daring reflect the Visionary Leader, yet whose day-to-day delight in tinkering with new ideas and improvising solutions betrays the heart of the Creative Alchemist. Or consider a founder who anchors a bold mission in pragmatic, community-building systems, embodying both Resilient Builder and Visionary Leader energies in equal measure.

In each case, the core gifts of two or more archetypes work in tandem, supplying both the spark of inspiration and the steady fuel required to carry that spark into reality. At the same time, the shadows of these archetypes can collide. A blended Visionary Leader/Creative Alchemist might dream vast new worlds only to see them stall for lack of follow-through; a Resilient Builder/Empowered Healer may devote themselves to community well-being yet become overwhelmed by the very networks they seek to nurture.

Recognizing these blended patterns becomes essential to conscious growth. When you observe which archetypal energies rise most strongly and how they support each other, and where they trip one another up, then you gain a nuanced roadmap for your own individuation process.

Discovering the Hidden Pattern

To bring your success archetype out of the abstract and into your daily practice, it helps to see concrete patterns in action which are rituals and routines that prime your unique energy for wealth creation. Here are illustrative success patterns for each of the four primary archetypes, followed by examples of how blended archetypes can craft hybrid routines that honor their multifaceted gifts.

The Visionary Leader thrives on clarity of direction and the inspiration of others. Each morning, set aside ten minutes to envision the next frontier you wish to conquer and whether it's a new market, a transformative product, or a cultural shift that you intend to spark.

Write this vision at the top of your day's to-do list, and then dedicate one "vision hour" in the afternoon to map progress against it. What small decisions today will bring that grand idea closer to reality? At the week's end, convene a brief "collective feedback" huddle to gather diverse viewpoints on your trajectory, ensuring your bold plans remain grounded in the insights of those you lead.

The Creative Alchemist flourishes when imagination and discipline dance together. Begin by carving out a daily "inspiration window" during which you explore new ideas without judgment by sketching, free-writing, or mind-mapping whatever arises.

Immediately afterward, commit to a short "execution block," where you translate one spark of inspiration into a concrete prototype or draft. To keep momentum, enlist a creativity partner. This peer will review your prototype at the end of the week, challenging you to refine and focus. Over time, these paired cycles of unbridled ideation and purposeful follow-through will turn whimsical notions into lasting innovations.

The Resilient Builder anchors lofty ambitions in steady progress and community engagement. Each Monday morning, conduct a "structural audit" of your projects: celebrate yesterday's small wins, identify one process to simplify, and plan two experiments to test in the coming days.

Midweek, host a micro-workshop with a trusted colleague or mentor, no more than thirty minutes long, to brainstorm adaptive pivots and troubleshoot bottlenecks. Finally, on Friday, send a "gratitude round" message to collaborators, acknowledging shared contributions and fostering the sense of collective momentum that fuels your enterprise's resilience.

The Empowered Healer turns generosity into sustainable abundance by balancing giving with receiving. Carve out a daily "compassion check-in" to journal how you have supported others and how you have supported yourself. Schedule two weekly "receiving rituals," such as accepting feedback from a client, inviting a supportive colleague to treat you to a coffee, or simply noting three genuine compliments you receive. By consciously toggling between outreach and intake, you reinforce the principle that self-care is the wellspring of generous service rather than an indulgence.

As I mentioned previously, most of us do not embody a single archetype in isolation. We're usually a dynamic blend of two (and sometimes more) archetypes. Each pairing creates its own flavor of strengths and challenges.

By crafting hybrid success patterns that honor these blended energies with the foundational archetype, you design a rhythm of work and reflection perfectly attuned to your unique profile. Imagine first the Visionary Leader/Creative Alchemist blend in which boundless imagination meets strategic foresight. Each week opens with a "macro vision session," projecting ten steps into the future by sketching the grand goals you long to see realized, only to follow each day with a focused "creative sprint," prototyping one tangible element of that vision. This alternating dance of expansion and contraction both keeps your bold ambitions alive and grounds them in the small, iterative acts of creation that bring possibility into form.

Now consider the Visionary Leader/Resilient Builder combination where daring ideas find their anchor in steadfast persistence. At the start of each month, you map new market frontiers and bold partnerships in a "frontier forecast," then translate those horizons into weekly "resilience rituals." These are structured experiments that test your hypotheses in the real world. When setbacks arrive, your builder side steadies the ship, while your visionary spark lights the way forward, ensuring that each challenge becomes the soil for your next advance.

The Creative Alchemist/Resilient Builder hybrid weaves innovation and structure so neither overwhelms the other. Mondays are set aside for "wild idea harvests," where every bold concept is harvested onto the page, while Wednesdays become "innovation checklists during which you choose one idea to systematize into a small pilot. By midweek, inspiration has been scaffolded into process, and by Friday, you debrief with your network, ensuring that each creative leap stands on a sturdy framework.

When imagination is paired with empathy, the Creative Alchemist/Empowered Healer emerges, channeling a creative spark into meaningful service. Your daily "inspiration practice" begins with a visualization of how your next innovation will lift lives, followed by an afternoon "reciprocity pause," actively inviting feedback or expressions of gratitude from those you serve. Over time, this blend ensures that each flight of fancy is tethered to human connection, transforming visionary ideas into authentic value that ripples outward.

In the Resilient Builder/Empowered Healer fusion, endurance and empathy converge to create both fortitude and compassion. Twice a month, you convene a "meeting of the minds circle," inviting colleagues or clients to share logistical hurdles alongside personal stories, weaving practical problem-solving with genuine emotional support. Each week, you follow this with a "boundary recalibration" ritual, pausing to examine where your generosity may have overextended you. You take the time to restore the balance between giving and receiving that sustains both the communities you uplift and you.

Finally, the Visionary Leader/Empowered Healer blend unites grand purpose with compassionate service. Each quarter, you host a "vision fair," presenting long-term goals to a circle of trusted allies and beneficiaries. Then, each month, you perform a "heart audit," reflecting on the emotional impact of your leadership choices to ensure your vision remains suffused with empathy. The pairing harnesses the power of big ideas to create tangible social good, keeping your drive both visionary and deeply human.

These hybrid routines do more than keep you busy. They train you to live precisely at the intersection of your archetypal gifts. Over time, as these success patterns become second nature, your archetypal blueprint will no longer operate behind the scenes. Instead, it will emerge as the conscious engine of your prosperity. You will get steered toward the right opportunities, fortifying you through inevitable challenges, and guiding you into a form of wealth that feels utterly authentic.

Yet even the most elegant blueprint can only reach its full potential when every element of its design, from the brightest gifts to the darkest shadows, has been acknowledged. Fully activating your success archetype therefore calls for a final, courageous step: bringing that shadow side into the light, where its unconscious impulses can be transformed into conscious strength.

Dialogue With Your Shadow

Engaging in a genuine dialogue with your shadow may feel unsettling at first and as though you are speaking aloud to a hidden companion you've long kept at arm's length, but it is precisely this kind of courageous inquiry that dissolves unconscious resistance and paves the way for lasting transformation.

Begin by creating a calm, focused space. Settle into your favorite chair, and take several slow, grounding breaths until your body and mind feel centered. Then imagine the aspect of yourself that most yearns for integration and the shadowed layer of your success archetype is seated across from you. If you recognize yourself primarily as a Visionary Leader, you might see this shadow as the part of you that hoards authority, convinced that only you can chart the right course. Ask aloud, "What do you fear would happen if I trusted others to share in this vision?" Listen with curiosity, not judgment, as your shadow responds, perhaps in words, in images, or in the body sense of tension or relief. In your journal, note the precise posture, the tone then finally the emotion you observe. For example, "My shadow leaned back with folded arms and whispered, 'If I let go, we'll lose control and the whole journey will derail.'"

For the Creative Alchemist, your shadow may appear as a restless spark, leaping from one idea to the next to avoid the discomfort of completing any single project. Pose the question, "Why do you keep chasing new sparks when so many dreams remain unfinished?" Attend to the resistance, the hesitation, or even the excitement that surfaces, writing down every nuance as though transcribing dialogue.

When your dominant pattern is the Resilient Builder, your shadow might manifest as a cautionary voice demanding certainty before every leap. Gently ask, "What holds you back from embracing the unknown?" and observe how your shadow's reply of "I need security, or we risk collapse" reveals both a protective instinct and self-imposed constraint.

If you identify most with the Empowered Healer, your shadow may take the form of martyrdom. You may hear an inner voice insisting that self-sacrifice is the truest measure of value. Question it softly: "Why does giving so much feel like the only way to prove my worth?" Notice the sorrow or urgency in its answer, then capture that precise language in your reflection.

Because most of us are complex blends of archetypes, you can also engage hybrid shadows. A Visionary Leader/Creative Alchemist blend might wrestle with the impulse both to command and to chase every new inspiration without follow-through. You could ask, "What am I afraid will be lost if I slow down and share control?" and listen for dual fears of diluted vision and of an incomplete creation.

A Visionary Leader/Resilient Builder fusion might confront the shock of unplanned upheaval asking, "Why do I cling so tightly to plans when life demands flexibility?" In each case, your written dialogue reveals how layered fears intertwine.

The Creative Alchemist/Resilient Builder shadow may hold two stories at once, one urging boundless novelty and the other demanding perfect structure. Invite it forward with, "How can we honor both discovery and finish line?" and witness how your shadow negotiates the tension between chaos and order.

A Creative Alchemist/Empowered Healer shadow might whisper that your imaginative gifts only count if they serve others perfectly. Ask it, "Why must every idea be a cure, and what happens if I imagine just for joy?"

A Resilient Builder/Empowered Healer blend may sit between rigorous problem-solving and total self-sacrifice. You might ask, "What fears drive me to both protect and exhaust myself?" and write down the dual longing for safety and for connection that surfaces. Finally, a Visionary Leader/Empowered Healer combination often struggles to reconcile big-picture ambition with compassionate presence. Ask, "How can I think boldly without leaving compassion behind," then honor the wisdom of both capacities as it speaks.

Once this initial exchange settles, take a quiet moment to sift through the truths it revealed. How have these competing values shown up in your past and perhaps driven you to push forward at the cost of relationships, or pulled you back so you never quite realized your full potential?

To cement this integration, choose a weekly ritual—maybe over morning tea or before you rest at night—to revisit your dialogue with the shadow and note what unfolded in your experiment. Did proposing an audacious goal inspire fresh enthusiasm without alienating anyone? Did the listening circle reveal ideas that refined your direction and deepened commitment?

Closing Remarks:

As we draw this chapter to a close, remember that your success archetype rendered vivid through rituals, reinforced in your daily habits, and fully enlivened by shadow dialogue that serves as both compass and engine on your journey to wealth. No longer a hidden pattern, it becomes a conscious ally, illuminating your strengths, alerting you to blind spots, and empowering you to step confidently into each unfolding opportunity.

Yet even the most integrated blueprint harbors corners still veiled from view. Deep within us lie repressed financial beliefs and the fear of scarcity, shame around abundance, or the lingering conviction that "I don't deserve this." These shadowed convictions can subtly erode our progress, whispering doubt when our archetype calls us to expansion. In Chapter Four, we will turn our full attention to these hidden barricades. Through targeted shadow work, we will unearth the unconscious money stories that keep you small, confront the repressed beliefs that undermine your confidence, and replace them with a robust financial growth mindset. By shining light on these shadows, you will liberate the last reserves of your potential and transform limitation into leverage, fear into fuel.

CHAPTER FOUR

The Shadow of Wealth: Breaking Financial Limitations

"The shadow is a tight passage, a narrow door, whose painful constriction no one is spared who goes down to the deep well."

— *Carl G. Jung, Aion: Researches into the Phenomenology of the Self*
(Collected Works, Vol. 9, Part II)

The moment you first glimpse your success archetype and begin practicing success patterns, you take a profound step toward wealth that is sustainable. Yet even the most refined blueprint for prosperity can be thwarted by unseen forces lurking in the shadows of the psyche that can repress financial beliefs. Such shadows show up as unexamined fears of abundance or most commonly, the limit stories inherited from family.

In Jungian terms, this is the realm of the shadow of wealth which is the cluster of unconscious attitudes that quietly undermine our efforts while masquerading as circumstance, or just "bad luck."

According to my investigation and study of Jungian concepts, to break free from these financial limitations, we must shine the light of consciousness into the darkest corners of our money mindset. This is shadow work or rather a courageous, skillful excavation of the beliefs we have buried, the guilt we carry when we think of earning more than we "deserve," and the scripts that tell us wealth is for "others," not for us. When we refuse to look honestly at these shadows, they continue to steer our choices and ultimately divert our success. Overcoming them is not optional; it is the very gateway to the abundance we seek.

The Origins of Financial Shadows

Long before we ever budgeted or negotiated a salary, our earliest experiences with money quietly wrote the prologue to our financial story. Perhaps your parents cautioned you that scarcity lurked around every corner, coupling "We don't talk about money; it's too risky" with displays of genuine love that essentially were instilling the paradox that discussing abundance threatened the very bonds meant to nurture you. You may have watched a grandparent suit up in frugality like armor, each saved penny a talisman against an imagined future of want. Perhaps you grew up in a community where wealth was synonymous with moral decay, teaching you that comfort carried the taint of selfishness and that true virtue lay in subsisting on the barest essentials.

According to Jung, these early messages become what he called emotionally charged constellations of thoughts and feelings that have split off from conscious awareness and taken up residence in the personal unconscious. A wealth complex, then, might carry the encoded belief, "I am not worthy of abundance," or "Rich people are corrupt," operating beneath the threshold of everyday thought. When such complexes remain unexamined, they exert a magnetic pull-on behavior. You set audacious goals in daylight only to shrink from opportunity at dusk, undercharge despite excellence, or feel inexplicable panic as your bank balance swells.

Jung also taught that these personal complexes are mirrored in the collective unconscious, the deeper layer of the psyche where universal archetypes dwell. Across cultures and centuries, money myths have carried similar shadows. By acknowledging that our personal money fears partake of these timeless themes, we not only validate their power but also open the door to transforming them. Shadow work is the process by which we retrieve these disowned parts as well as those hidden beliefs and fears that have secretly dictated our financial choices, then we invite them back into conscious dialogue.

This is not an exercise in self-flagellation; it is a demonstration of Jungian courage and curiosity. We illuminate the sting of "I don't deserve this" so that we might rewrite it into "I am worthy of abundance and will use it wisely." We honor the protective instinct that equated surplus with danger, then guide it to see wealth as a resource for growth rather than as a threat to stability. In doing so, we transform what is hidden into consciousness, and the very energies that once undermined our prosperity become the fuel for our wholeness. Only then can true wealth flow, un-shadowed, through every decision we make.

The Inner Critic

At the heart of this transformation lies a familiar yet formidable foe: the inner critic. As the shadow of wealth's most common emissary, it murmurs at the back of your mind, doubting every move and predicting every failure. When you contemplate asking for a raise, it recalls that purchase you regretted last year; when you pitch a bold project, it dredges up a long-forgotten rejection. Left unchecked, this inner critic doesn't simply whisper in your ear. It also writes the script you follow, steering you toward cautious incremental gains instead of the exponential growth you're capable of.

To confront your inner critic, begin with simple awareness. Spend several days journaling its monologues verbatim, including every taunt or every warning. Then note the physical sensations you feel like the tightness in your chest or for some it's the heat in your face. For others there may be a slump in your shoulders. By capturing both the words and the bodily reactions, you give form to something previously vague.

Next, give it a name—perhaps "Mrs. Caution" or "Mr. Undeserving"— so that you can externalize the voice and see it as one part of yourself, not the whole. Once you've mapped your inner critic's terrain, it's time for a gentle interrogation. When it declares, "You don't deserve that raise," counter with three concrete examples of the unique value you have delivered. When it warns, "Wealth will isolate you," bring to mind friends and mentors who have celebrated your success and stood by you through change. This exercise won't silence the inner critic permanently. However, it will transform it into a balanced advisor and one that acknowledges risk without extinguishing your ambition.

As you continue this practice, certain rules of thumb can help you manage your inner critic more effectively:

• Schedule a daily "worry window." Give your critic five minutes to voice all its concerns, then close the journal until the next session. This contains negativity in a fixed time, freeing the rest of your day for constructive action.

• Ask, "What's the worst that could happen?" Then, plan a small, concrete response to that scenario. Often the critic's greatest fear turns out to be manageable once it is spelled out and addressed.

• Practice self-compassion affirmations. After every journaling session, speak kindly to yourself. Say something like, "I did hard work by confronting these fears." This soothes the nervous system and reminds you that inner conflict is part of growth.

• Frame setbacks as data. When a critic-predicted failure does occur, treat it as information rather than proof of unworthiness. Ask, "What can I learn from this?" before returning to action.

Over time, the inner critic's voice will lose its power. Its warnings become prompts for inquiry, not immutable decrees. As the dialogue between your conscious ambition and your shadowed fears deepens, you will discover that every doubt carries a hidden gift: a lesson in humility, an opportunity for refinement, or a reminder to anchor your vision in values that sustain you. With each exchange, your inner landscape grows richer, and the path to true financial freedom becomes ever clearer.

Guilt is another shadowy force that shackles our financial potential. Thoughts such as, "How can I enjoy luxury when others are struggling?" or "If I profit, am I robbing someone else?" are not rational obstacles but deeply felt complexes lodged in your unconscious.

Jung observed that, until these moral complexes are brought into consciousness, they exert their power invisibly, casting a long shadow over every decision and keeping you trapped in half-measures of generosity and ambition alike. To loosen guilt's grip, you must undertake a radical reframe. Understand that wealth is not a zero-sum game. Instead, it is a dynamic resource you can multiply and share. When you prosper, you create new possibilities with funding ventures that employ others, supporting causes you believe in, or simply freeing yourself to give in ways you could never attempt under scarcity's yoke. Each act of generosity fueled by real abundance sends ripples far beyond your own circle, proving that prosperity grows when it is released and not hoarded.

In my research, one practical rule of thumb I found for dissolving guilt is the "Moral Ledger" exercise. At the start of each week, quietly list five recent instances in which your work or investments have contributed positively to others' lives. For example, maybe it was mentoring a colleague by guiding them through a process for starting a business. Perhaps it is setting up a networking opportunity with some key investors. Seeing your generosity recorded in black and white reminds you that your wealth already lifts others, balancing the ledger of your conscience and making space for healthy self-interest.

Another helpful practice is the "Permission Slip." Each morning, craft a single sentence that serves as your permission statement—for example, "I allow myself to earn abundantly and to use that wealth to expand the good I can do in the world." Write it on a sticky note, and place it where you'll see it (at your desk, on your bathroom mirror, etc.). Each time guilt tugs at you, glance at your permission slip, inhale deeply, and repeat the words on it aloud.

With every utterance, you rewire the neural pathways that once linked abundance to shame, replacing them with associations of empowerment and service. You can also embrace a "Celebration Budget" which is setting aside a small, guilt-free allowance each month for personal enjoyment. This can be a dinner out at your favorite restaurant or a weekend excursion that promotes relaxation. Before you spend, pause and ask yourself, "How will this choice nourish my creativity, my gratitude, or my relationships?" If the answer resonates, proceed with confidence. Over time, you'll discover that joy need not be earned through sacrifice. Rather, it can be a catalyst for greater generosity and innovation.

Finally, practice compassionate inquiry whenever guilt arises. Instead of pushing the feeling away, lean in and journal a brief dialogue. Ask the part of yourself that feels guilty, "What do you need me to understand?" Then listen for its answer or for its fear of judgment or a warped sense of responsibility, and respond with kindness: "I hear you, and I choose to act with integrity and joy." This gentle back-and-forth dialogue transforms guilt from a paralytic force into a guide, illuminating the values you most want to uphold.

By weaving these practices into your daily life, you transform guilt from a shackle into a signal and one that alerts you when your choices stray from your highest purpose. And as guilt recedes, permission takes its place, allowing you to receive abundance with the same grace you extend to others, thereby completing the cycle of giving and receiving that lies at the heart of true financial freedom.

Transforming Scarcity Into a Growth Mindset

Scarcity thinking is the belief that "there's never enough." In Jungian terms, scarcity is complex and born of early emotional imprints that have crystallized into a self-perpetuating myth. Jung described complexes as clusters of feelings and thoughts that operate outside our conscious intention; the scarcity complex siphons energy into hoarding safety rather than cultivating possibility. To dispel its shadow, we must first shine light on these unconscious patterns, lifting them into conscious exploration.

Begin by noticing the physiological markers of scarcity: the tightening in your chest when you hear of a competitor's windfall, the restless need to check your bank account after every transaction, or the sudden chill when you imagine saying "yes" to a new investment. Jung taught that bringing sympathetic attention to these somatic signals, or what he might have called the "body's unconscious language," is the first step toward integration.

Once you are alert to a scarcity trigger, pause and consciously reframe the narrative. Instead of letting, "There isn't enough" echo in your mind, cultivate the question, "How can I create more value?" In place of the fear, "I might lose everything," invite curiosity: "What can I learn from this experience, regardless of outcome?"

Over time, these repeated linguistic transformations become new neural pathways, rewiring your default orientation from defensive contraction to creative expansion. This is not mere positive thinking. It is a process akin to Jung's concept of individuation, whereby we integrate unconscious contents into the living tapestry of consciousness. Each time you consciously choose a growth-oriented response, you weaken the scarcity complex, reclaiming energy that once went into limiting beliefs and redirecting it toward innovative action. In this way, financial challenges cease to be threats and become invitations to cultivate abundance.

Shadow Dialogues for Financial Freedom

Deep shadow work often unfolds through structured inner dialogue and what Jung might have termed active imagination, a technique for giving voice to unconscious figures until they can be consciously assimilated. Imagine convening an internal symposium in your mind's theater. One by one, invite your "Scarcity Self," your "Guilt Guardian," and your "Inner Critic" to speak into the quiet room, while your "Curious Observer" listens without judgment.

Ask each part to reveal its deepest concern: "Why do you believe wealth is dangerous?" or "How have you protected me through these warnings?" Listen without rushing to rebuttal; allow each voice to express its fear or intention fully. Then, shift roles and respond from your wise self which is that integrated center Jung described as the Self, where conscious and unconscious meet. Offer empathy: "I understand your care to keep us safe. Thank you for watching over me." Introduce new information grounded in reality: "Economic data shows that value creation can expand resources for many. We can contribute to that positive cycle." Finally, invite collaboration: "Let us work together to build abundance responsibly."

Journal these exchanges in detail, assigning each voice a name and persona to deepen the sense of real dialog. Over weeks, this practice dissolves the opposition between your protective shadows and your creative aspirations, weaving them into a cohesive team whose combined insights guide every financial choice.

Rituals for Embracing Abundance

Jung understood ritual not as empty repetition, but as a sacred act and one that bridges the invisible realms of the psyche with the tangible world of form. When approached with intention, ritual becomes a language through which the unconscious speaks and transformation takes root. In the journey of financial individuation, rituals serve as living symbols, reinforcing the inner work of shadow integration by giving it a rhythm in your outer life.

Begin each morning in stillness, whether you simply place a hand on your heart or create a space where intention can surface. Let your first breath be a quiet invocation: "I release the scarcity within and welcome the flow of wealth." Speak it aloud or within, not just as affirmation, but as an energetic commitment. Feel the sound resonate through your body. Let the sound become a mirror of your inner shift or a moment where fear dissolves and receiving begins.

Midweek offers a chance to reconnect with your value. Pause to reflect on how you've contributed, not only through tasks, but through presence. Consider the client who left your meeting lighter or the colleague who benefited from your encouragement. Think about the quiet courage it took to hold a boundary or take a leap. Don't overlook these moments, because they are evidence of worth in motion. Jung taught that true consciousness arises from the integration of thought and feeling, and this practice is precisely that: a harmonizing of inner purpose with outer expression.

As the week closes, turn your attention to what arrived without force. Revisit moments of unexpected grace: a conversation that opened a door, a new idea that sparked at just the right time, a synchronicity that felt like life answering your desire. These are not mere coincidences, but they are signs that abundance is already in motion, responding to your inner alignment. By noticing them and offering gratitude, you gently retrain your nervous system to trust in the flow of provision.

With time, these rituals become more than habits. They evolve into sacred rhythms that mark your calendar with intention. Each reflection that you journal becomes a declaration that wealth is not a destination or a stroke of luck but, rather, a relationship and the outward expression of your integrated self. Through these simple acts, you transform the shadow into fuel used for converting resistance into rhythm. Fuel that can transform scarcity into a steady embodied trust that abundance is the present you now claim.

As you begin to unravel the shadow of wealth, you may come to a striking realization. What once felt like a fixed destiny is not fate. It is a script written in childhood, passed down through cultural norms and family legacies that quietly runs in the background of your financial decisions.

In Jungian language, these are complexes. They are emotionally charged clusters of belief and behavior, exiled to the personal unconscious yet echoing deeper archetypes from the collective. To move beyond these inherited roles is to step into individuation. Once again, this is the lifelong process Jung described as becoming whole by making the unconscious conscious. And in the realm of money, this process is revolutionary. It means having the courage to face the voices within you that say, "You're not enough," "You don't deserve more," or "Abundance will change you for the worse."

These aren't enemies. They are loyal messengers from your past, trying to protect you in outdated ways. When you engage them in dialogue or when you ask them what they fear, what they need, and what they've been trying to guard, you begin to shift from self-sabotage to self-leadership.

Through rituals of reflection and practice, these inner shifts become lived experience. A morning mantra becomes a statement of identity. A midweek reflection on the value you've added affirms your worth beyond numbers. A weekend audit of unexpected blessings helps reorient your nervous system from vigilance to trust.

Over time, old beliefs loosen their grip. The thought, "There's not enough" transforms into "How can I create and share more?" The reflexive guilt of "I shouldn't want this" evolves into "I am allowed to prosper, and my prosperity has a purpose."

You begin to claim space in alignment with your truth. This is the essence of a financial growth mindset. It is not a hustle or a hype. It is a deep, inner reorganization. It is the integration of mind and heart, insight, and embodiment.

You start to see setbacks not as signs to stop, but as moments to adapt. Money is no longer just a currency, but it is viewed as energy that reflects your inner state and your evolving contribution to the world.

As Jung once wrote, "The greatest and most important problems of life are all fundamentally insoluble." We are not meant to solve them like equations, but to engage them and to live into them with presence, curiosity, and courage.

This mindset shifts you from bracing against life to collaborating with it. You are no longer driven by fear of loss or shame about wanting more. Instead, you approach each financial choice with integrity and possibility. Wealth is no longer a prize for the deserving few. Instead, it is a natural outcome of wholeness. It flows from coherence and when your conscious aspirations are in conversation with your deeper psyche, and every part of you, even the shadowy ones, has a seat at the table.

Closing Remarks:

As you cross the threshold from this chapter into the next, take a moment to honor how far you've come. You've ventured into the depths of your financial unconscious. You've named your hidden beliefs, listened to the fears behind your resistance, and begun to reframe your story by integrating it rather than erasing the past. In doing so, you've initiated a sacred alliance between your inner world and your outer results.

This is not just about money. This is about becoming someone who can hold more abundance without collapsing into old patterns. You are now cultivating a state of being where wealth is welcomed from wholeness rather than pursued from lack.

In Chapter Five, we will explore how both literal and psychological symbols can anchor this new mindset. But, before you turn the page, breathe. Feel the strength it took to do this inner work. Take a moment to feel the depth of self-honesty and the vulnerability of truth with the willingness that was required to meet your fears with grace.

These moments are not small. They are the quiet revolutions that change everything. Stand here, in the light of your awareness, and remember this: There is no shadow too dark to integrate nor belief too deep to rewire. The wellspring of prosperity is not a destination. It is a more conscious, more courageous and more whole you than you've ever been.

CHAPTER FIVE

The Power of Symbolism in Financial Mastery

"Man lives in a world of meaning. What we see and experience is not just matter, but symbol."
—*Carl Jung*

Before you ever touched money, before you could articulate your dreams of success or safety, you lived in a world shaped by symbols. As a child, wealth wasn't numbers on a spreadsheet. It might have been the sound of your parents arguing behind closed doors about budgeting, the sensation of envy when someone else had more, the warmth of a rare luxury, or the emptiness that followed its absence.

Money became a symbol long before it became a tool, and that symbolic weight continues to shape your financial choices in ways that remain largely unconscious. Jung believed that the psyche does not speak in rational language alone but, rather, in images and symbols.

In Jungian terms, symbols are not mere signs. They are dynamic vessels of energy and meaning. Jung believed that they arise from the unconscious, carrying with them both personal significance and archetypal resonance. He wrote that symbols can heal or haunt, or inspire or imprison, depending on how we engage with them. And, in the realm of wealth, symbols are everywhere. They are hidden in the stories we tell ourselves, the rituals we practice, the objects we cherish, and the patterns we repeat.

Money is never just money. For many it is the key to dreams and the root of anxiety. It is both the promise of tomorrow and the echo of yesterday's fears. In the Jungian sense, this makes money one of the most potent modern archetypes which is a collective projection of our deepest psychological energies. The dollar, the contract, and the title deed are not only instruments of trade but are also sacred tokens in our inner mythologies.

Perhaps you grew up with the silent symbol of an empty fridge or a worn-out wallet, internalizing the message that wealth is elusive and always just out of reach. Or maybe you inherited a talisman of prosperity like your grandfather's watch, perhaps even an inheritance that carries not just value but the weight of expectation.

In either case, the symbol holds more than substance; it holds story. To master money, you must first master the meaning you've assigned to it. Jung taught that to individuate, we must recognize and integrate the symbols that live within us. They are clues from the unconscious, each one offering a pathway to greater self-awareness. In this way, financial mastery becomes not merely about strategy. It becomes about soul. It is less about managing your net worth and more about understanding your inner wealth narrative.

Cultural and Ancestral Symbolism of Money

To fully understand the symbolic power of money in your life, you must look not only within your personal psychology but also behind you. What I mean is look into the long corridor of your cultural and ancestral inheritance. Jung taught that our unconscious is not formed in isolation. It is shaped by both the personal unconscious, the sum of our individual experiences, as well as the collective unconscious, the deep psychic reservoir of humanity's shared archetypes and ancestral memories.

Nowhere is this inheritance more potent, or more unexamined, than in our inherited beliefs about wealth. In some lineages, wealth is seen as divine favor, a sign of spiritual alignment. In others, it is regarded with suspicion or as the fruit of exploitation or even a curse passed down through broken moral codes.

These cultural interpretations live on not just in textbooks but in the quiet, subconscious ways in which you react to money today: the guilt you feel when you earn more than your parents did, the anxiety you inherit from generations that lived through war or displacement, even the secret belief that "people like me don't become wealthy" whispered down the family line like a spell.

This is not merely social conditioning. It is psychic symbolism. As Jung observed, ancestral experiences, particularly those charged with emotion or trauma, can be passed down as complexes. These complexes form invisible patterns in the psyche that may no longer match your present reality but still govern your financial decisions.

Perhaps you sabotage new opportunities because a great-grandparent once lost everything. Or you cling to money with iron fists because scarcity was your family's dominant myth. These inherited emotional truths form part of your inner money map, and until you bring them into your consciousness, they will shape your financial destiny more powerfully than any spreadsheet ever could.

To transform your wealth psyche at the symbolic level, you must become an archaeologist of your own financial lineage. Ask yourself: What was the emotional atmosphere around money in my home growing up? What financial traumas or triumphs marked my ancestors' lives? What cultural values shaped how wealth was spoken about or not spoken about at all?

In doing so, you begin to see that what you thought were personal money beliefs may, in fact, be archetypal legacies or cultural and ancestral narratives still playing out in your life. The gift of this awareness is that it allows you to consciously choose what to carry forward and what to lay down.

You are not fated to repeat the past. The symbolic chain can be rewritten. Jung believed that healing happens not by rejecting the unconscious, but by integrating it or by shining the light of awareness on the shadow and finding new, life-giving meaning.

In this context, rewriting your financial story is not about rebellion; it is about reclamation. You reclaim the right to believe that wealth can be sacred, that money can be used in service of wholeness, and that abundance reveals rather than corrupts.

As you engage with the cultural and ancestral symbols that shaped your relationship with money, you are doing more than self-reflection. You are performing an act of psychic liberation. You become the living bridge between the past and the possible. Through intention and symbolic reinforcement, you can craft a new story and one that honors the struggles of those who came before, while stepping boldly into a future they may have only dreamed was possible.

Using Symbolic Reinforcement to Transform Your Wealth Psyche

It's not enough to think positive thoughts about money or mentally affirm your worthiness of abundance. Lasting transformation takes root only when those thoughts are embodied and when they are anchored through symbols that speak directly to the unconscious. This is not mysticism; it is the psychology of meaning-making. As Jung emphasized, "The symbol is the best possible expression for something unknown." As I stated earlier, prior, symbols allow you to communicate with parts of your psyche that reason alone cannot reach.

Think of a wedding ring. On the surface, it's a simple object a metal shaped into a circle. But through intention, ritual, and repetition, it becomes infused with meaning. It becomes a promise and a sacred declaration. Your relationship with wealth can be infused with that same depth of symbolic meaning.

The key is to recognize that your unconscious is always watching and always listening. It pays attention not only to what you say, but also to what you do. It studies the way you shape your environment and the signals you send about what truly matters.

Start with your environment. Look around you. What does your current financial landscape say about how you perceive wealth? Is your wallet a chaotic jumble of receipts, torn at the seams, and forgotten at the bottom of a bag? Is your desk cluttered with unpaid bills or unopened statements? These may seem like mundane details, but they are symbols. They speak volumes to your unconscious, reinforcing narratives of avoidance or neglect.

By consciously upgrading your financial environment, you send a powerful message to the deeper parts of yourself that "Wealth is safe here. Wealth is welcome." Choose a wallet that feels worthy of the energy you wish to invite. Keep your workspace tidy and intentional. Use financial tools that evoke clarity rather than confusion. These are not acts of vanity; they are acts of symbolic affirmation.

You might also design what Jung might have called a "symbolic container," or a vision ledger or financial journal that is more than just a budgeting tool. Fill it not only with numbers but also with desires and images that evoke the archetype you wish to embody.

Over time, these symbols form a kind of psychic scaffolding. They retrain your emotional responses. The mind begins to associate financial activity not with threat or shame but, instead, with presence and possibility. This is symbolic reinforcement at work. It is where ritual meets neurology, where story meets structure, and where shadow meets soul.

And perhaps most subtle, yet most powerful of all, is your language. Words are the most immediate and accessible symbols we use, and they hold tremendous influence. When you say, "I can't afford that," you are not simply stating a fact, but you are reinforcing a symbolic identity of limitation. Replace that with, "I choose not to invest in that right now," and you shift from victimhood to agency. One phrase closes doors; the other opens them.

Jung believed that language, when imbued with archetypal force, had the power to awaken and transform the psyche. Every sentence you speak about money, whether aloud or silently, either reinforces your scarcity complex or nurtures your wealth archetype. Choose your words as if they are sacred incantations, because to the unconscious, they are.

In this way, symbolic reinforcement becomes a daily art form. It is not about perfection. It is about consistency coupled with intention. With each word or gesture, you teach the unconscious that abundance is not only desired, but it is deserved. You are no longer just earning; you are embodying prosperity itself. Each action becomes a reminder that wealth is not outside of you, but alive within you.

You are transforming your relationship with wealth from something merely transactional into something deeply transformational. In Jungian terms, this is individuation in action. Which is the gradual weaving together of the symbolic, the emotional, the behavioral, and the spiritual into a coherent sense of self. When you engage with symbolic reinforcement, you don't just change your finances. You also evolve into the kind of person who can steward wealth with clarity.

The Soul of the Symbol

To live a financially symbolic life is to return to reality at its deepest layer. It is to recognize that beneath the surface of every monetary act lies a network of values and beliefs that shape your decisions and your very identity. Jung taught that symbols are not mere signs, but they are also psychic organs. He describes it as dynamic and alive, growing as we grow, and they are capable of transforming our consciousness if we learn to engage with them intentionally.

In this light, financial mastery is not just about numbers, but it is about reshaping the symbolic language your psyche uses to understand power and worth. Every dollar you earn or spend carries the echo of your personal mythology. It is not neutral. It is a story in motion. A paycheck may symbolize stability or self-worth. A gift may speak of generosity or an unconscious attempt to win approval. A financial risk might represent courage or a hidden compulsion to escape stagnation.

When you live symbolically, you begin to see these transactions as messages instead of as events. You ask not only, "What am I doing with my money?" but also, "What is my money trying to show me about myself?"

This is the soul of the symbol in financial life. It is the recognition that wealth is always standing in for something deeper. The dollar in your hand is a placeholder for autonomy. The savings account is a modern talisman for survival, echoing ancient instincts. The investment portfolio becomes a metaphor for faith in the future. Money becomes a mirror, reflecting your inner world and your outer choices. And, like all mirrors, it can distort your reality unless approached with consciousness.

Jung believed that symbols were the means by which the unconscious speaks to us. They emerge from the dreams you have or the synchronicities that you experience. Jung also mentioned that the unconscious communicates to us in our daily patterns often carrying messages from the hidden self to the waking mind. When you begin to engage with money symbolically, you open that channel. You begin to see your financial life as a dream rich with metaphor. Is your checking account always empty just before abundance arrives? That might not be mismanagement alone. It could be a pattern repeating or an old wound around lack and last-minute survival.

These symbols, when interpreted with compassion, become initiations. A once-feared symbol—for example, asking for more money, raising your rates, or charging what you deserve—can, through the alchemy of awareness, become a sacred act. What once triggered shame can now become a rite of reclamation.

A misunderstood archetype much like the "greedy rich person" you were taught to despise might, when you re-examine it, reveal a deeper archetypal calling like the magician who multiplies resources for the benefit of all.

The ultimate symbol in financial life, however, is not the dollar or the ledger or the stock chart. It is the narrative you carry within the myth you live by. This is what Jung called the personal myth or, rather, a private constellation of symbolic meaning that gives your life coherence. What is the myth you've inherited around money? Is it one of endless struggle? Sudden loss? Punishment for success? When you become aware of the symbolic threads running through your financial life, you can begin to consciously reweave the story.

Perhaps wealth, for you, has long symbolized survival to get by. But what if that symbol evolved? What if it came to represent getting free instead of just getting by? Not just consuming, but creating? Not just safety, but sacred service? This shift is not merely mental. It is symbolic. And it is extremely transformative.

When you begin to reshape your internal mythology around wealth, you are no longer unconsciously reacting to the past. You are consciously co-creating the future. Symbolism in financial mastery is the art of turning numbers into narratives and scarcity into soul work. It is how the outer world of money becomes a living metaphor for your inner journey. It is how you begin to see that prosperity is a dynamic process that is an ever-evolving conversation between your conscious goals and unconscious truths rather than a destination.

In this conversation, symbols are your language. And when you learn to read them, your financial life becomes more than management. It becomes meaning. To live symbolically means to walk through your financial world as a sacred landscape. This means seeing your receipts as records of your values and your spending as self-expression. It also means to see, even in your debts, the call to become someone larger than your past. This is not theory. This is soul in action. This is your wealth becoming alive. And, as Jungian concept would remind us, the more consciously we engage with the symbol, the less we are ruled by it. So, the more meaning we bring to money, the more meaning money brings to us.

Closing Statement:

To live symbolically with money is to choose presence over performance. It means relating to wealth not as an object to control, but as an archetype to honor. Receipts become records of your values. Income reflects your contribution. Spending reveals your self-expression. Even debt can be understood as an initiation into your next chapter. In this light, money is no longer a battleground, but it becomes sacred ground."

This is not abstraction. This is soul in motion. This is the mythic dimension of financial mastery. As Jung so wisely taught, "We do not become enlightened by imagining figures of light, but by making the darkness conscious." You are doing just that, bringing light to the unseen symbols that have governed your financial life. You are reclaiming the projections, rewriting the inherited myths, and recoding the language that once kept you small. You are transforming money from a shadowed symbol of lack into a conscious ally of your purpose.

We arrive at a new horizon. This is the moment where symbolism meets strategy and where inner alignment meets outer expression. In the next chapter, Success Patterns, we will leave the inner sanctum of the psyche and step into the daily practices that give shape to your symbolic breakthroughs.

Because mastery is not born only in insight but, rather, in repetition. And ritual. And movement. There, in the rhythm of intentional habits, your archetypal stewardship will take root in the soil of real-world action. But, for now, breathe. Let this chapter settle in your bones. Take a moment to feel the shift in how you view money and how you understand your money story. You are no longer just earning a living. You are living a symbol. And, in doing so, you are becoming the author of a new legacy and one in which wealth is no longer a symbol of fear but, instead, a language of soul.

CHAPTER SIX

The Psychological Laws of Success and Failure

"Man's task is to become conscious of the contents that press upward from the unconscious."

—Carl Jung

Success and failure are not merely outcomes but instead they are reflections. They mirror the invisible architecture of our psyche: the beliefs we hold, the patterns we repeat, and the myths we live without knowing.

As we move from symbolic understanding into the terrain of tangible results, it may be tempting to believe we are now dealing solely in logic and strategy. But understand that our external realities continue to be shaped by internal truths.

Even in the practical realm of money, the unconscious remains our most powerful ally or our most subtle saboteur. In the previous chapters, we explored how money serves as a potent symbol charged with personal meaning. We examined how our rituals and language influence our relationship with wealth. Now, we step into a more dynamic space: the psychological engines that drive success or quietly engineer failure.

In my continued investigation, this is where symbols become strategies and where self-awareness must meet action. At the heart of this exploration lies Jung's concept of the collective unconscious which was previously mentioned in other chapters as an inheritance shared by all human beings, filled with archetypes that form the structural DNA of the soul.

It is here, in these unseen layers of mind, that we find the roots of our self-sabotage patterns, the recurring blocks that seem to defy logic or intention. Why do we resist opportunities that could liberate us? Why do we repeat financial missteps despite knowing better? Why does the fear of success, or the weight of unworthiness, so often shadow our most promising moments?

Jung never saw failure as merely circumstantial or random. He saw it as an expression of the unconscious or a symbolic gesture of the soul, attempting to make itself heard. Failure is often a message we haven't yet learned to decode. Likewise, true success is not a lucky accident nor is it solely the result of grit. It is a psychological alignment between our conscious desires and our unconscious permissions. Without this alignment, progress remains partial.

This chapter is not a map of tactics but, rather, of inner laws that I have pieced together from psychological principles that govern the success or failure of our outer pursuits. We will look closely at self-sabotage, not as a flaw to be eradicated, but as a language to be understood. We will decode behavioral finance, not just through economics, but also through archetypes and emotional histories. And we will walk the narrow but luminous path of individuation which, again, is Jung's term for the lifelong journey toward wholeness, as it expresses itself in our financial and vocational lives.

To succeed in the truest sense is to become more fully yourself. To fail consciously is to grow wiser. Each has its role in your evolution. But to do either, unconsciously, is to repeat the same chapter under a different name. Let's look deeply at not just what we want but also at what within us resists what we want. Only by turning inward can we break the invisible patterns that keep success at bay and claim the version of life we are truly meant to live.

Self-Sabotage: The Shadow's Dance

Jung famously described the shadow as the part of the psyche we deny, often containing aspects of ourselves that are unacceptable. While commonly viewed as "negative," the shadow is not inherently bad; it is simply unconscious. And what remains unconscious wields great power over us.

In the realm of finances, the shadow often dances in the form of self-sabotage. We find ourselves repeating patterns that seem irrational or destructive: procrastinating on taxes, undercharging for our work, chronically overspending, or avoiding wealth-building altogether.

But these behaviors are not accidents. They are not mere laziness or lack of intelligence. They are expressions of inner conflict. The psyche, when burdened by unresolved emotional material, finds subtle and symbolic ways to protect itself, even if that protection comes at the cost of success.

Take, for example, the individual who earns well but always ends up in debt. This may not be due to ignorance but to a deep, unspoken belief inherited from family or culture that wealth is selfish. Or consider the entrepreneur who sabotages each opportunity at the moment it could succeed. Beneath this pattern may lie a shadow belief that visibility is unsafe, that abundance invites judgment, or that failure is more familiar and, thus, more comfortable than transformation.

These inner saboteurs arise from complexes or emotionally charged mental structures that Jung described as splinter personalities within the psyche. A money complex might be formed by childhood experiences of scarcity or even ancestral trauma. Such complexes act autonomously and, until we bring them into consciousness, they repeat themselves across a lifetime, creating outcomes we consciously try to avoid.

Jung emphasized that the first and most important step toward healing is awareness. By bringing these hidden patterns into the light of consciousness, we remove their grip over our lives. Integration of the shadow does not mean eradicating these parts of us. It means understanding and embracing them.

When we give voice to the part of us that fears wealth, we begin a dialogue that leads to healing. When we acknowledge the part of us that feels unworthy, we start the process of reclamation. Financial self-sabotage, then, is not a moral failing. It is the soul's cry for integration. It is a signal that some part of us has not yet been allowed to be known.

The goal is not to dominate or suppress these parts, but to evolve with them from fragmentation to wholeness. Only then can our outer financial world become a reflection of our inner coherence. The key, as Jung reminds us again and again, is that what we do not make conscious will rule us from the shadows.

The Law of Inner Opposition: Success Awakens the Counterforce

If you have ever found yourself on the cusp of a breakthrough or about to close the deal, only to feel anxiety rise like a tide, you have touched the first law: success awakens its opposite. Jung called this phenomenon enantiodromia or the principle that, when a force reaches its extreme, it inevitably engenders its opposite. What begins as bold momentum can just as quickly become its inverse.

And this reversal isn't arbitrary. It is the psyche's deep-seated effort to restore balance. In Jungian terms, the ego identity may be reaching forward into a new possibility, a new role, or a new sense of power. But the unconscious, rooted in history, may perceive this expansion as a threat. The psyche remembers every time you failed, were punished for shining, or saw someone fall from success.

And so, when you strive toward growth, a counterforce awakens, not to destroy you but to protect you. This action, I have come to realize, is not sabotage out of malice, but protection out of memory. This is our mind's paradox. You long for abundance, visibility, and purpose yet, when the moment comes close, you tremble. Something within you braces. And this is the moment where most turn back. They take the resistance as a sign that they've overreached.

But Jung would insist the opposite. He would say that the presence of resistance is not proof that you're on the wrong path. Instead, it's confirmation that you're touching your psychic edge. During my research, I discovered that the psyche does not resist what is familiar, but it resists what is transformative. To evolve, you must become aware of this inner opposition and recognize this not as a flaw but as a rite of passage.

The doubt or sudden inertia you feel at the brink of success is the psyche equivalent of altitude sickness. You are ascending a new psychological mountain, and your inner system must adjust to the thinner air of a new identity.

So, how do we overcome this? Well, not by force and not by denial. We overcome these situations by inner opposition or by making it conscious. So, self-sabotage or procrastination, it is all a message, not a mistake. Ask it questions: What part of me is afraid of this next level? What belief would this success contradict? Whose voice inside me doubts I am worthy of this? What would I have to let go of if I allowed this success in fully?

This is the beginning of what Jung called shadow integration which we touched on in previous chapters. The shadow is not inherently dark; it is simply what we do not yet own. And, for many, the shadow contains not just fear but also power. It encompasses the fear of shining, and the fear of responsibility as well as the fear of surpassing our parents, our culture, or our old identities. These are ancestral echoes we carry unconsciously.

Sometimes, the inner opposition arises not because success is wrong but because we are attempting to achieve it without inner permission. A part of you may not yet feel safe being seen. A younger self within may not yet believe they deserve more. An old wound may whisper, "If you win, you'll be alone." These are not fantasies. They are all a part of the innerworkings of the psyche.

I have discovered that, to overcome them, you must renegotiate those psyche patterns or beliefs. This means ritualizing your transition into success, and not just strategizing but psychologizing it. Create intentional time to grieve the identities you are leaving behind. Take time to grieve the version of yourself that survived on scarcity or even martyrdom. Give them a symbolic burial and invite the new self forward—not as an intruder but as a rightful heir.

The deep work of transformation involves changing your behavior and expanding your identity to include the very qualities you once feared. Jung reminds us that "you do not become enlightened by imagining figures of light, but by making the darkness conscious." In other words, you will not transcend the resistance, but you must include it. You must learn its language and ultimately, its limits. Because here is the truth of the Law of Inner Opposition: The moment you turn toward the resistance with curiosity instead of fear, it loses its grip. The shadow stops being a saboteur and becomes a guide.

The resistance, once integrated, becomes fuel. Success is not achieved by suppressing the counterforce, but it is earned by learning how to hold it, speak with it, and grow beyond it. This is how you evolve. This is how you win, not just externally, but at the deepest psyche level. This is how you become the kind of person who can reach success and sustain it.

The Law of Psychic Compensation: What You Refuse, Rules You

Jung observed a profound and immutable truth about the human psyche: it longs for balance. This isn't balance in the superficial sense of scheduling work and rest or counting calories, but an archetypal equilibrium between the conscious and the unconscious.

This drive toward balance is not a passive state but an active psyche mechanism that Jung called psychic compensation. At its essence, psychic compensation is the psyche's attempt to correct one-sidedness. If the ego over-identifies with control, then the unconscious will begin to stir with symptoms that oppose it. This is not punishment; it is simply nature.

The psyche is self-regulating. It does not tolerate extremes without consequence. And nowhere is this more evident than in the pursuit of financial or worldly success. You may believe you are failing at discipline when, in fact, your deeper self is intervening. You may think you lack drive when, in truth, your psyche is rebelling against a path that denies your creative nature. Please note that the burnout or the strange coincidences that pull you off track are not random.

They are symbolic. They are messages from self. To understand this law is to awaken to the startling realization that what you repress does not disappear. It governs you from the shadows. If you deny your hunger for wealth, perhaps due to inherited beliefs that money is corrupt, then it may express itself as resentment toward others who have what you will not allow yourself to desire. If you suppress your need for rest, the body may fall ill. If you suppress ambition, it may contort into passive-aggression or even depression. The unconscious never forgets. Instead, it compensates, and it always seeks wholeness.

In Jung's view, symptoms are not errors. They are communications. The psyche speaks in dreams, synchronicities, and even financial patterns. A string of missed opportunities may be a reflection of inner dissonance rather than bad luck. A repeated pattern of gain followed by loss may signal a part of you that feels unworthy of success. These are not financial flaws. They are psychological compensations, requesting your attention. To heal this, we must do something profoundly difficult in modern culture. We must slow down and listen to what the symptoms are saying.

This is where transformation begins. Ask yourself: What part of my nature have I disowned in my pursuit of success? Have I become so focused on doing that I've forgotten being? What old belief am I secretly living out that no longer matches my truth? Where is life forcing balance upon me? Is it through crisis, through exhaustion, or through financial instability all because I refused to create it voluntarily? This is the emotional alchemy Jung spoke of: becoming conscious of the unconscious so that it no longer controls you from the dark.

Integration is the cure. You must bring in the neglected part. If you've been all will and no feeling, then invite intuition back into your decision-making. If you've worshipped productivity, allow yourself to daydream, and to do nothing, and see what new direction emerges. If you've clung to humility to the point of self-erasure, dare to speak your name and claim your space in the world.

This is not arrogance; it is restoration. The being you are does not want you to succeed in half-light. It wants you whole. The Law of Psychic Compensation is not here to punish but to protect the integrity of your being. When you ignore it, it whispers. When you resist it, it disrupts. But when you hear it, it reconciles. Success built on compensation is fragile. But success built on integration on all aspects of your inner life has the stability of self, being, and soul behind it.

You overcome this law by honoring what has been pushed away rather than by pushing harder. The solution is not always more effort. Sometimes, it is more honesty. More awareness. More compassion for the neglected parts of yourself that, though inconvenient, are utterly essential.

As Jung wrote, "The most terrifying thing is to accept oneself completely." Yet that is the invitation here. Stop fighting the parts of you that threaten your success and begin weaving them into a larger, truer, more sustainable version of it.

In this light, failure is not always defeat. Sometimes, it is the psyche rescuing you from a life that would have cost your wholeness. So, the question becomes this. Are you willing to succeed in a way that includes all of you? Are you ready to let yourself, being, or soul's longing become part of your financial strategy? Because when you do, success becomes more than achievement. It becomes integration. It becomes peace and, from that place, absolutely everything becomes possible.

The Law of the Transcendent Function: Wholeness As the New Wealth

In Jungian psychology, the transcendent function represents one of the most sacred and complex processes of inner development. It is not a mental trick or productivity hack. It is the psyche's alchemy through which opposing forces within the self are reconciled, not by domination or denial, but through dialogue. It is the hidden mechanism that allows a person to evolve beyond the limitations of contradiction. When engaged, it gives birth to an entirely new level of being or an expanded state of consciousness in which authenticity and expansion can finally coexist. This function is "transcendent," because it enables us to rise above the conflict that divides us internally. It integrates, rather than splits.

This is the true key to lasting success and not superficial wins. It is a kind of existential coherence, where what you desire, what you believe, and how you behave are no longer at war with each other. Consider the inner conflicts so many feel—for example, the desire to build wealth while fearing that money might corrupt their integrity or the urge to pursue visibility and leadership while harboring unconscious fears of being judged or abandoned.

These contradictions don't mean you're broken. They mean you're alive and human. The problem arises when we try to resolve these paradoxes by choosing sides. We either abandon our ambition in the name of spiritual purity, or we abandon our soul in the name of success. Either way, we fracture. Jung believed that wholeness is not found in extremes but, rather, in the tension between them.

To engage the transcendent function is to stay with the discomfort of the paradox and not to solve it prematurely, but to honor both sides of the psyche until a third, previously unimaginable path reveals itself. This is not an intellectual process but an experiential one. And it begins with your willingness to stop rushing to answers. Instead of asking, "How do I get rid of this conflict?" ask,

"What does each side of this conflict need me to understand?" Ask, "What part of me wants success and what does it imagine it will cost? What part of me craves safety and what does it fear will happen if I grow?"

In the space between these opposites, something sacred begins to stir. That stirring is the transcendent function at work. A new symbolic image may arise in a dream; a synchronicity may confirm the path your mind doubted; and a feeling of internal clarity might settle in your body before you've made a single external change. These are not coincidences. They are signs that your inner life is coming into alignment.

To foster this process, you must create space physically and also in the mind. Please note that reflection, therapy and meditation are not indulgences that are mentioned over and over by other great leaders in the psychology field. They are the tools by which you hear the unconscious speak. Symbolic rituals matter here, too. A letter written to self can become a symbolic acts that signal to the unconscious you are ready for integration.

Jung emphasized that the psyche responds to what is lived, not just what is thought. That means showing up to the paradox not with answers, but with reverence. The gift of the transcendent function is not simply "solving" your problem. It is allowing you to become someone who no longer needs the same problem to grow. The contradiction that once felt like a block becomes a threshold. The impasse becomes initiation.

From this space of integration, you begin to build success that is not stolen from parts of yourself but is constructed with all of you. There is no more winning at the cost of your well-being. There are no more passion projects starved of profit. You begin to feel your goals as extensions of your whole being, not as performances for external approval. You move through life with less resistance, because you are no longer divided. Instead, you are aligned and no longer chasing or hiding but becoming.

Success born from this level of integration is transformational and sustainable. A milestone is reached as you meet your whole self. You begin to lead from performance as well as from presence. You no longer fight your inner world to earn your place in the outer one. Then finally, you understand that your psyche is not an obstacle to success, but it is the instrument of it. So, if you find yourself in contradiction just know that you are on holy ground. The transcendent function is alive in you, working in the background, and preparing the soil for a new consciousness to emerge.

Let it. Nourish it. Stay with it. You do not need to be less divided to begin. You only need to become more aware because, when your success includes your whole self, then the shadow will no longer need to be chased.

Closing Statement:

Success, as we now understand, is not a stroke of luck or a product of relentless hustle. It is the natural outcome of a psyche that has been harmonized and where the conscious and unconscious work not in conflict but in communion. When your inner world is fractured, even the most sophisticated strategies fracture with it. But when your inner world is whole, even small steps create seismic change.

Jung taught that what we fail to make conscious appear in our lives as fate. In the realm of wealth and achievement, this means that every repeating financial struggle and every pattern of sabotage is not random. It is the psyche calling you to awareness. It is your unlived life asking to be known.

We've now explored some of the deepest psychological concepts that govern your relationship with success and failure. We have learned together that success or failure are not imposed by society but etched into the human psyche. The law of Inner opposition shows us that success will always awaken a counterforce, but that resistance is a gateway rather than a wall. The law of psychic compensation reveals that the parts of ourselves we reject will rule our behaviors from the shadows until we invite them into the light. The transcendent function reminds us that by holding opposing truths in tension, we make space for the emergence of something entirely new.

These laws are not meant to be feared. They are meant to be worked with, like tools. And once you know how to listen, you stop fighting your patterns and start deciphering them. You stop fearing failure and start honoring it as feedback. You stop worshiping surface-level success and start pursuing a success that is both externally impactful and internally aligned.

Now, as we prepare to move forward, the question becomes: how do we bridge this inner mastery with external creation? How do we translate symbolic insight and psychological wisdom into real-world wealth? How do we apply the truths of the unconscious to the systems of manifestation, belief, and behavioral change?

In the next chapter, we will shift from the archetypal to the actionable. You will understand why wealth creation is not a vague mystery but, rooted in identity, coherence, and energetic precision.

If Chapter Six taught you how to see the unconscious patterns shaping your life, Chapter Seven will teach you how to rewire them and manifest by design. This is where the science meets the soul.

CHAPTER SEVEN

Manifestation or Mindset? The Real Science of Wealth Creation

"Your vision will become clear only when you can look into your own heart. Who looks outside, dreams; who looks inside, awakes."
—*Carl Jung*

In nearly every book or coaching session on wealth manifestation, the formula remains remarkably consistent: visualize your desires, align emotionally, speak affirmations, act as if it has already happened, and trust the universe. These methods, often popularized in mainstream teachings, are not without merit. They've helped countless individuals shift from scarcity to abundance and from confusion to clarity.

But there is an essential piece missing from this formula and one that explains why so many people can manifest something extraordinary, only to sabotage it rapidly. The missing key is not more belief or hustle. It's not about doubling down on vision boards or perfecting your scripting rituals. The missing key is integration. And this is where Jung's depth psychology opens a radically new dimension and the path from manifestation to what I call Sovereign Manifestation.

We are often taught that manifestation and mindset are two different things. We are taught that the former is magical thinking while the latter is hard-nosed psychology. But, in truth, they are two sides of the same internal equation. Manifestation is the outward expression of your inner architecture. Mindset is the blueprint. You don't manifest what you say you want; you manifest what your subconscious has accepted as familiar.

Without inner receptivity, manifestation techniques remain performative. And, without mindset work, the unconscious cannot support the vision. Even when results appear, they are often temporary, because the person has not become sovereign enough to hold them. Mainstream manifestation encourages you to "act as if." But sovereign manifestation requires something bolder: to "be as is"— not to perform a frequency, but to inhabit your truth so fully that the external world begins to reflect your inner coherence. This is where Jungian psychology becomes essential as a framework for sustainable expansion rather than as a spiritual novelty.

Jung did not speak directly of wealth, but he gave us tools to sustain powerful transformation. His concepts of the transcendent function, active imagination, and archetypal alignment are not abstract theories; they are scaffolding. They ensure that you become someone who can house what you've summoned.

Becoming a Sovereign Container

The transcendent function, as explored in previous chapters, refers to the psychic mechanism by which the conscious and unconscious parts of the psyche integrate, creating a "third" position. In the context of wealth, it helps you reconcile old, embedded identity patterns like "I'm not worthy of success" or "Wealth corrupts" with the emerging reality of prosperity.

Without this reconciliation, success may arrive, but the psyche won't know how to hold it. Self-sabotage follows, not as failure, but as protection from the incongruence between your inner world and outer reality.

This is where mainstream teachings fall short. They celebrate the moment of attainment but ignore the psychic aftershock. Jung understood, as few coaches do, that the psyche demands congruence. If you manifest a million-dollar business while still carrying unconscious shame about being seen, or guilt about surpassing your family, then you've planted seeds of internal collapse.

The psyche is a container for truth rather than a stage for performance. To bridge this gap, we must go beyond manifestation into psychological sovereignty. Sovereignty in this context means authorship of your inner world. It is the ability to remain whole in the face of expansion rather than reverting to old beliefs when new realities stretch the limits of your self-concept. It is not dominance. It is integration. It is the Self, but with a capital S. Essentially, taking authority over your psychic landscape.

Sovereign manifestation is not merely about getting what you want. It is about becoming someone who can live with, lead with, and grow with what you've created. It moves manifestation from a fleeting victory into a sustained evolution.

The Neuropsychology of Sovereign Manifestation

At the core of sovereign manifestation is a regulated, coherent self and not a fragmented psyche striving to control outcomes. This is where mindset becomes neurological. The brain must interpret wealth and success as safe to sustain. Otherwise, it will activate primitive defense mechanisms: fight, flight or freeze.

No vision board can override a nervous system in survival mode. Most people sabotage their manifestations not because they aren't deserving, but because their biology perceives expansion as a threat. They've been unconsciously conditioned to associate wealth with disconnection and power with abandonment. For many, these associations are not conscious thoughts but are stored somatic memories that were encoded in the body long before the conscious mind formed beliefs about success.

This is why mindset must go beyond cognitive reframing and into the body. You cannot think your way into safety. You must feel your way into safety. Sovereign manifestation acknowledges this biological and psychological reality. It doesn't just affirm wealth, but it also conditions the nervous system to feel safe enough to live with it. This is an act of neuro-symbolic integration. It means retraining the subconscious and somatic mind through safe success experiences and emotional reconsolidation.

This is why mindset work isn't about motivation. It's about regulation. It's not about chasing high-frequency states but about building nervous system capacity to hold complexity without collapse.

The human nervous system is built for familiarity, not fulfillment. It seeks what's known and not what's best. If wealth feels unfamiliar at a nervous system level, the brain will trigger subtle forms of sabotage to restore its sense of psychological safety. These sabotages can manifest in the form of: You'll "forget" to follow up on opportunities or you procrastinate right before your business launch. These are not mindset failures. Instead, they're somatic coping mechanisms.

To rewire this, you must deliberately normalize expansion. That means exposing yourself gently and intentionally to the very things you fear will destabilize you. By doing this, you will integrate a deeper sense of safety into your body as you step into new dimensions of your life. This work is less glamorous than achieving overnight results, but it is far more sustainable. It's what turns manifestation into a stable lifestyle, not a temporary miracle.

This is why rewiring is a sovereign act. It is a deliberate reconfiguration of how you relate to power and your place in the world not just in thought but also in presence. You must build new internal associations to understand that wealth is nourishing, not isolating. That visibility is connection, not exposure. That power is service, not threat.

Mainstream manifestation teaches us to perform success to act "as if," dress the part, say the affirmations, and visualize the desired outcome. While these strategies can initiate momentum, they often create a split between who we are and who we're pretending to be.

The result is spiritual perfectionism masked as progress. You become fluent in the language of abundance, but internally, you're tense, hypervigilant, and over-identified with performance. You start micro-managing your every thought: Am I resisting or blocking? But underneath that striving is often a core fear that you're still not enough and that you must earn your manifestations through spiritual compliance.

Sovereign manifestation invites something far deeper—to be as is rather than to act. To stop performing a frequency and, instead, become the truth of it. Essentially, build a mindset that no longer needs to micromanage the universe because your internal state has become a stable match for what you desire. This isn't about blind faith. No, it's about inner coherence.

In sovereign mode, you are no longer chasing a reality. You are radiating one. You are not manipulating outcomes. Instead, you are embodying stability. You've become the kind of person reality trusts to reflect with generosity, because you no longer fear what you're calling in. And how do you become that person? By building the internal conditions where expansion doesn't cause fragmentation. Where receiving doesn't trigger collapse. Where success feels safe.

This is the true mindset of sovereignty and not rituals of pretend alignment, but nervous system coherence. Psychological congruence. Truth. Safety in the Self. Because the truth is that you don't manifest what you want. You manifest what your system believes is safe to receive. If abundance feels like abandonment, then your body will reject it, no matter how perfectly you say your affirmations. If visibility feels like vulnerability, you will unconsciously shrink when opportunities arise. This isn't a block. It's biology doing its job.

So the task isn't to override your fear. It's to rewire it. To create small, repeatable experiences of success that don't overwhelm your system but, instead, anchor new emotional truths including: You are not unsafe with money. You are not disloyal for being powerful. You are not unlovable if you rise.

This is the inner work of sovereign manifestation. And when that internal alignment stabilizes, something remarkable happens. You stop chasing results, and you start becoming results. Reality organizes around you, not because you said the right words but because you became the right container. Your manifestations stop being spikes. They become settled states. Your nervous system no longer sabotages the expansion. Instead, it supports it.

This is the future of wealth creation: Not performance but presence. Not manicured alignment but lived and embodied coherence. When the mindset becomes sovereign, manifestation becomes inevitable. This happens because you become someone who can live with what you called in.

Sovereignty Alignment: Rituals of Inner Stability

Every act of manifestation either aligns with or conflicts with the archetypes you are currently inhabiting. These archetypes are universal patterns of identity and energy that are not just poetic ideas or spiritual concepts. They are psyche blueprints, shaping how you experience power and purpose.

When these archetypal forces are unconscious or unintegrated, they don't disappear. They direct your life from the shadows. Archetypal alignment, therefore, is not aesthetic. It's foundational. It's the psychological architecture that determines whether your success feels like embodiment or exile.

This brings us to the practice of sovereignty alignment, or a set of symbolic, psychological, and ritual methodologies designed to maintain congruence between your evolving outer world and your inner truth. Manifestation may begin with desire, but it is stabilized through sovereignty. And sovereignty must be maintained deliberately, or else the psyche reverts to familiar patterns that feel safer, even if they're smaller.

Sovereignty alignment is not a one-time act. It is a living dialogue or a conversation between who you were, who you are becoming, and the unconscious layers of self that still need permission to come along. These practices are the inner ceremonies of coherence. They allow you to integrate success not just into your calendar or bank account, but into your being.

One such practice is archetypal anchoring. This is the conscious return to the inner figure and the part of you through active imagination during your manifestation journey. Once your goal becomes real, your archetypal figure doesn't vanish. It must be re-engaged. Archetypal anchoring prevents your psyche from becoming outdated in the face of new success. It ensures your inner allies evolve with you.

Another powerful ritual is what I call thresholding or a ceremonial act of consciously crossing into a new identity. We often downplay transitions, treating them as merely logistical. But, psychologically, thresholds are potent. They mark the death of one identity and the birth of another. Whether you write a letter to your former self or consciously enter a new space—for example, an upgraded office, home, or financial status—with intention, the ritual sends a signal to the unconscious. We are no longer who we were. Still, this is safe. Thresholding doesn't just honor your growth. It also stabilizes it.

A third form of alignment is dream dialogue, or using dreams as post-manifestation feedback. Your unconscious speaks in symbols, not language. Once a manifestation becomes reality, the dream world often activates, giving you data on which parts of your psyche feel safe and which don't. Are you dreaming of losing things? Being exposed? Running late? These are not bad omens. They are invitations.

Your dreams expose where old patterns still reside. They also reveal where integration is needed, and where new power must be claimed. The bottom line is that manifestation is not a finish line. It's a doorway, and sovereignty alignment is the ritual of tending to what lives on the other side.

If you do not anchor the self, the shadow will do it for you. If you do not engage the unconscious, it will engage you and often through crisis. That said, sovereign manifestation requires ongoing alignment. Not perfection, but presence. Not force, but reverence for the evolving terrain of your psyche. This is how wealth becomes not a trophy but, instead, an extension of your truth.

Sovereign Manifestation: Holding the Crown

Sovereign manifestation is not just the next level of success. It is the maturation of the spiritual and psychological journey and a kind of sacred stewardship that begins when the applause fades and the soul whispers: now what? This is the phase most teachings ignore—not because it's unimportant, but because it's inconvenient. It doesn't sparkle like a vision board nor does it thrill like quick wins.

But it is the very phase that determines whether what you manifest becomes your foundation or your undoing. This deeper work begins quietly. Often, it begins in the stillness after the celebration, when the outer world finally matches your inner desire, and yet some subtle tremors arise. You wonder: Am I really allowed to have this? Without sovereignty, success doesn't feel like freedom. It feels like surveillance. You begin watching yourself, hyper-aware, afraid of losing what you've finally gained. You brace for the crash because your new identity hasn't yet been safely installed in the nervous system.

This is the unspoken weight of success. This is the crown. And, while many want to wear it, few are taught how to carry it—not just emotionally, but psychologically and somatically. The crown is not just a symbol of status, but it is also a pressure system. It magnifies who you are. If you carry unhealed shame, it echoes. The crown doesn't give you power. It reveals whether you've integrated it.

Sovereignty, then, is not found in the moment of triumph. It is revealed in how you walk with the responsibility of your own expansion, in how you handle visibility without crumbling, and in how you continue evolving, even as others place you on pedestals you never asked for.

This process is not linear. Sovereignty is not a badge you earn and keep forever. You evolve in spirals. Each new level of success brings new archetypal tensions and new shadow contents to meet. Without sovereignty, these spirals feel like regressions. You start to question whether you're "out of alignment" or "blocking abundance." But, with sovereignty, you recognize the truth is that you are integrating a larger life. You are becoming more whole. You are not falling apart but you are expanding your psychic container to hold more of who you truly are.

Mainstream teachings often tell you to hold the vision. But sovereign manifestation asks you to hold yourself—not just the parts that are lit up and ambitious, but also the parts that are scared.

These parts include the inner child who equated visibility with betrayal, the adolescent who believed wealth meant loneliness, and the parts of you still grieving an identity left behind. When you hold these parts with presence, you don't just create wealth, but you also embody it. You become rich in integration.

This is why sovereign manifestation is the future of wealth psychology. It bridges spiritual insight with psychological infrastructure. It doesn't just help you get what you want. It also helps you become someone who can live with what you've created without collapse. You no longer feel like an imposter in your own life. You feel like the architect of it. When this happens, something extraordinary occurs. You stop seeking confirmation from the outer world because your presence alone becomes the signal. This is what it means to hold the crown with confidence and with coherence.

Sovereign manifestation doesn't ask you to become perfect. It asks you to become present to your evolving self. This is not the end of your journey. It's the point where everything stabilizes into soul. This is the sacred art of becoming the one who can keep what they create—not just for a season, but for a lifetime.

Closing Statement:

Sovereign manifestation is the return to the seat of your own authorship. The rituals, recalibrations, and rewiring you've encountered in this chapter are not techniques to perfect. They are inner technologies to live by. You are not here to perform a life of success. You are here to embody one with integrity, with inner safety, and with sovereign authority. As we close this chapter, remember that manifestation without mindset is fantasy. Mindset without integration is limitation.

When manifestation, mindset, and sovereignty meet, you become the architecture of wealth itself. You stop chasing outcomes and start commanding reality through coherence. This means that you no longer strive to hold the crown. You are the crown that is rooted. The journey forward is not about having more. It is about becoming more yourself.

CHAPTER EIGHT

The Code of Wealth–Aligning Action With Intuition

"The pendulum of the mind oscillates between sense and nonsense, not between right and wrong."
—Carl Jung

To understand the true art of wealth creation, one must go beyond logic. The hidden architecture behind sustained prosperity is not just discipline or hustle. It is something far more elusive.

It is intuition. In Chapter One, we introduced the concept of the code of wealth, a symbolic and psychological framework that governs how individuals interact with money, power, and identity. This code is not a formula to memorize but, rather, a living language to be deciphered. It moves through archetypes, symbols as well as energetic alignments. At the center of this code lies the compass of intuition.

Intuition, when properly understood, is not simply a mysterious inner feeling. It is the knowing that emerges when your psyche is aligned with truth. It does not arrive from panic or desire but from coherence.

In the world of finance, intuition is often dismissed as unreliable, yet some of the greatest entrepreneurs attribute their most successful decisions to a deep sense of inner certainty. This chapter explores the deeper science behind this certainty and offers a map for developing intuitive financial decision-making through archetypal alignment.

Jung, perhaps more than any thinker of his time, illuminated the structure of the inner world in a way that bridges mysticism with psychology. In his theory of psychological types, Jung identified intuition as one of the four primary cognitive functions alongside thinking, feeling, and sensation. Intuition, according to Jung, is the function that perceives patterns, and symbols without relying on direct sensory input.

The intuitive types do not require evidence to know. They do not trace their insights back to a linear cause. Instead, their awareness moves through the unconscious, perceiving a reality that is unfolding rather than fixed. In wealth creation, the intuitive function becomes a hidden asset. Where others see risk, the intuitive mind sees archetypal movement.

Yet intuition cannot be wielded recklessly. For it to become reliable, you must distinguish intuition from emotional impulse. Jung was clear about this and the fact that intuition, when undeveloped, can easily drift into projection. This is why many confuse fear or excitement with intuition, leading to decisions that later feel misaligned.

Developing intuitive accuracy, then, is not a shortcut. It is a practice of individuation or the art of becoming whole enough that your unconscious no longer sabotages your inner knowing but, instead, supports it. This is where archetypes return as guides. Every financial decision is a psychological mirror rather than simply a transaction. Beneath every action around money lies an archetype. They are psyche patterns that speak through our nervous systems, our dreams, our fears, and our desires.

To make intuitive decisions, we must recognize which archetype is driving us in the moment. Are we investing from the voice of the sovereign or the wound of the orphan? The code of wealth demands that we make these drivers visible. Intuition without archetypal awareness can lead to distortion. But intuition integrated with archetypal alignment becomes a form of genius. It becomes a compass that leads you through complexity without collapsing your coherence.

This brings us to a unique insight: financial decisions are symbolic acts. Each choice we make with money reflects our inner mythology. Spending impulsively may not be about desire at all but, instead, about trying to fill a void. Avoiding wealth may not be a value of simplicity but, rather, a protection against visibility.

Jung's concept of projection teaches us that, what we reject internally, we often assign to the external world. Money becomes a canvas for these projections. The market becomes a mirror. Intuition allows us to see through these layers and retrieve our projections. Then it invites us to pause before the transaction and ask: What part of me is speaking right now? What archetype is at play? What shadow am I avoiding?

Jung's The Red Book was not written for public consumption. It is a record of his inner journey through active imagination and his dialogues with archetypal figures, his descent into the symbolic underworld, and his search for psychic truth. What emerges from this intimate text is not just the brilliance of Jung's inner vision but, also, the practice of intuitive integration.

Jung did not create his theories from detached study; he lived it. He recorded dreams, he dialogued with images, and he mapped his inner conflicts. In this way, the Red Book becomes a metaphor for wealth work. Your financial life is not just a series of spreadsheets or bank statements. It is your Red Book that contains your fears, your ambitions and your miracles.

To make intuitive financial decisions—to ask, "What should I do" and "Who am I becoming"—is to open the pages of your own Red Book. Wealth becomes less about acquisition and more about becoming the person who can hold what they've created with integrity. Intuition is the instrument for this becoming, and it tunes us into the deeper symphony of our psyche, allowing us to hear when we are in harmony and when we are out of tune.

Yet even intuition has a shadow. When distorted, it masquerades as an impulse. Pseudo-intuition can be just as seductive as the real thing. You may feel a jolt of urgency and mistake it for divine timing when, in truth, it is trauma reactivation. You may interpret resistance as misalignment when, in fact, it is the soul asking you to grow.

This is why sovereign manifestation must include the discipline of discernment. Not all inner voices are equal. Some must be loved but not obeyed, while others must be challenged. The question is not just to understand what your intuition is telling you but, also, to know which part of yourself is speaking, and what do they need to feel safe, heard, and whole?

The sovereign path is not one of blind surrender to instinct. It is the cultivation of psychic maturity. Jung's individuation process is not about perfection. It is about wholeness which is the ability to hold tension, to discern archetypes, to engage both shadow and light without collapse.

In the context of money, this becomes a holy discipline. It is the skill of becoming financially intuitive without bypassing the deeper work. Developing trust in your intuitive voice requires more than inspiration. It demands practice, and you must engage with your inner world as actively as you engage with your investments. This is where a technique like active imagination becomes practical.

Before making a significant financial decision, close your eyes. Visualize the moment as if it were a dream. Ask the inner figure who appears, "What do you want me to know?" Don't control the image. Let it speak. If a figure emerges, don't banish it. Listen. Integrate. These inner dialogues will tell you more about your financial alignment than any trend forecast or algorithm. As you cultivate these practices, the code of wealth begins to reveal its deeper meaning. It is not about mastering external wealth alone, but it is also about embodying the archetypal architecture of inner abundance. You become someone whose decisions are no longer ruled by panic or performance but, instead, by precision and the precision of a psyche that has become whole.

Intuition, in this context, is not a gift. It is a result. It is what happens when the self is no longer divided against itself. When what remains is your shadow and it is no longer in hiding, and your inner archetypes are no longer at war. This is the real intelligence behind wealth. It isn't just strategy or mindset. It is intuition made sovereign and action made symbolic to then identify as whole. That is the code of wealth fully awakened.

However, knowing the code is not enough. To live it, you must embody it. The real question becomes, how do you live a life where your inner archetypes, intuitive intelligence, and decision-making patterns remain aligned, even under uncertainty? How do you maintain clarity when money challenges arise, or when you're called to make the kind of financial leap that stirs your old fears back to life? The answer is not acquiring more knowledge but gaining deeper presence.

Living the code of wealth requires continual inner listening. This is not the same as analysis, and it is not obsessive thinking masked as planning. It is the disciplined act of becoming still enough to hear the inner voice. This is why true financial intuition cannot exist without inner archetypal literacy. You must know who is speaking within you. You must become a skilled interpreter of your own symbolic landscape, and above all be able to distinguish between trauma's urgency and the psyche's clarity.

This is the difference between a panic-based pivot and a soul-guided risk. One is reactive while the other is revelatory. Here is the paradox: The more you align with your archetypal truth, the less noise you encounter in your decision-making. You need less to outsource your power to experts or to trends. This is not because you become arrogant but, rather, because you become internally attuned. You still learn from others, and you still study the terrain, but the final vote belongs to your sovereign self.

When this shift takes place, wealth stops being the result of effort and starts emerging from elegance. Your financial choices begin to feel intentional rather than strained. Opportunities no longer need to make logical sense; you sense them before they arrive. You respond not from fear of missing out, but from an inner confirmation that feels precise and undeniable. That knowing isn't luck. It's the code of wealth speaking through you.

To become proficient in identifying the code, you must practice and recalibrate continuously. Even a sovereign identity can get weary, especially when facing failure, criticism, or even the unknown. This is why ongoing symbolic rituals matter along with the conscious revisiting of your archetypal roles. Another aspect is to also regularly have an inquiry into your financial patterns to ensure your not falling back into old patterns. Lastly, reflect on journaling after key decisions in order to extract feedback.

These practices are not just mental hygiene; they are also sovereignty maintenance. This is also where your dreams, synchronicities, and emotional triggers become rich data points. These data points are so essential because they reveal when you're slipping out of alignment. For example, a recurring dream of being chased may not just be random fear. It may be your sovereign urging you to stop abandoning your role. A synchronistic meeting with a stranger who mentions the exact investment you were hesitating about may not be coincidence but, rather, confirmation that you're on the right track. Even a moment of financial sabotage, like missing a deadline or avoiding a necessary conversation, isn't necessarily just procrastination. It may be an archetype crying out for safety.

To live the code of wealth is to live in dialogue with these messages, not in denial of them. This is not about being mystic for the sake of mysticism. It is about precision. Because in a world filled with noise, the wealthiest people are not those who accumulate the most information. They are those who discern which signal matters. That signal is often internal, archetypal, and unspoken until you've cultivated a strong enough relationship with your unconscious to hear it clearly.

When action and intuition become allies, you stop reacting and start resonating. You're no longer trying to force results. Instead, you respond to what is already emerging. In this state, intuition becomes less a feeling and more a frequency. Action transforms into embodiment. This is what it means to walk with the code and not as theory, but as lived truth.

Closing Statement:

To close this chapter, let us return to the one truth that threads through every intuitive decision, every archetypal alignment, and every act of courageous wealth-building. The fortune you generate in the external world is always in direct proportion to the clarity you have with your intentions. It is also the coherence and courage you cultivate within.

To be clear, it is not the absence of fear that marks the sovereign path. It is the presence of alignment despite that fear. The other point is that it is not about ever making mistakes, but about how swiftly and honestly you return to your center when misalignment is revealed.

Sovereignty is not perfection. It is precision of being and self-authorship without self-abandonment. The truly wealthy are not those who never doubt. It is those who no longer obey doubt as if it were law. They have trained themselves to hear the voices of uncertainty and yet move forward with integrity. They do not wait for absolute certainty to act; they act from a deeper certainty that lives beneath logic which is an embodied knowing.

That knowing is intuition, and when intuition is honored, strengthened, and defined through archetypal self-awareness, it becomes the compass for a new kind of prosperity. It is not performative wealth but, rather, living wealth.

In the end, wealth is not a destination to arrive at but, rather, a reflection that reveals itself moment by moment. It mirrors your inner world even if you experience order or inner chaos. It also reveals how fully you are living from truth and alignment with the self that Jung so deeply trusted to guide each of us into our unique destiny. That is the code of wealth, fully activated. It is not a rigid system. It is a living intelligence. It is not a formula but, rather, a frequency.

CHAPTER NINE

Archetypes in Action and Rewiring Your Mind for Financial Success

"In all chaos there is a cosmos, in all disorder a secret order."

—*Carl Jung*

There comes a moment on the path to wealth when strategy is no longer enough. You read the books, followed the advice, and made the investments that promised momentum. You even shifted your mindset and practiced visualizing success with crystal clarity. Yet something within still presses the brakes. That is the threshold where you encounter the true gatekeepers of your financial destiny which are the inner archetypes, long buried in the psyche, stirred awake by the charge of possibility.

This is the terrain of depth work. And here, in the invisible architecture of your inner world, lies the true secret to lasting financial transformation. It's not in control but, instead, in integration. It isn't in suppression but, rather, in dialogue.

While individuation has often been described as a personal journey or the integration of one's own unconscious, Jung also warned of the danger of ignoring the collective unconscious in times of cultural upheaval. He noted that, "the bigger the crowd, the more negligible the individual becomes."

In the realm of wealth, this has profound implications. Most financial systems today are built upon a collective mythos that was forged in centuries of hierarchical power and scarcity-based models. These economic blueprints did not arise randomly. They are psychic structures, encoded over generations through cultural archetypes that remain largely unchallenged. Individuation, in its truest and boldest form, must therefore include not only personal liberation from these inner complexes, but also a breaking of unconscious contracts with inherited collective roles. This is where wealth creation takes on moral and mythological dimensions.

To rewire your mind for financial success in a sustainable, soul-aligned way, you must investigate not only your subconscious, but the collective one you've been unknowingly participating in. Ask yourself, "What myth of money has my culture trained me to uphold? Who benefits from this narrative, and what part of me has been exiled in order to conform?"

This is no longer just shadow work. This is systemic individuation where the archetypal distortions of an entire economic era begin to collapse under the weight of growing consciousness. For instance, the archetype of the self-sacrificing healer, common among therapists and spiritual entrepreneurs, often unconsciously carries the collective myth that, to serve others, one must suffer or remain poor. Or the hyper-masculine achiever archetype, often embodied by founders or Wall Street elites, may operate from a shadow animus that equates domination with safety and visibility with invincibility, rooted in survival-era collective programming.

These are not simply character flaws. They are inherited masks, patterns passed down through generations under silent cultural contracts. They shape the way you approach money, influencing how you price, how you invest, even how you give or withhold. When you begin to examine these roles within yourself, it becomes clear that much of your financial behavior is not truly yours. It is the echo of ancestral memory and societal scripts playing through you.

This realization is liberating, and it creates a crack in the internalized system. It allows something new to enter. Jung believed that the psyche evolves in spirals and that integration is never a final state but, rather, is an ongoing recalibration. When we apply this idea to financial individuation, we come to understand that wealth is not just something we earn, but it is also something we remember. It is something we retrieve from the collective forgetting and reforge in the fires of intention. This leads us into a new concept: the symbolic wealth reclamation.

Turning Personal Integration Into Collective Liberation

Symbolic wealth reclamation is the process of reauthoring and reintegrating the archetypal energies you previously exiled through personal or collective trauma around wealth. It is the sacred act of taking back inner authority from outdated systems and infusing the financial field with new symbols rooted in wholeness.

This reclamation may begin as personal. It may involve claiming the right to raise your rates without guilt or allowing yourself to receive abundance without hustle. But it doesn't stop there. It evolves into a responsibility to seed new archetypes into the cultural field and embodied models of success that include psychological integrity. In doing so, you are not just building wealth, but you are also initiating a cultural individuation process by becoming a living counter-symbol to the myths that once governed your financial decisions. Jung warned that a culture without new symbols becomes neurotic, caught in loops of decay.

So, we must ask: What new symbols of wealth must now emerge? What archetypes are waiting in the collective unconscious, longing to be shared? I propose the emergence of four new archetypes for the next evolution of wealth consciousness. The first is the Sovereign Listener. This is the one who no longer leads through force but, instead, through deep attunement to truth. Their wealth is not manufactured but, rather, magnetized. It arises from the quiet authority of alignment. The sovereign listener hears beyond noise whether in market trends or inner dialogue and trusts resonance over rush. In their world, abundance follows coherence.

Then comes the Integrated Architect which is a visionary driven by the duty of building root structures that reflect wholeness instead of egotistic ambition. This archetype knows that true success is about soul and not about scale. Whether constructing a business, a brand, or a legacy, the Integrated Architect honors inner values as the blueprint. They are building to embody rather than to impress.

The Sacred Merchant also emerges in this new era. Often misunderstood, this archetype reclaims commerce as a spiritual exchange. The Sacred Merchant knows that selling, when done with clarity and integrity, is elevation rather than manipulation. They understand that wealth can be reciprocal in the long run when done from this point of view. Every transaction becomes a ritual of mutual empowerment, by which promoting a vote for a new kind of economy where honesty is a force multiplier rather than a liability.

Finally, we welcome the Embodied Oracle, or a decision-maker who walks the line between logic and intuition with sovereign grace. This archetype values data and structure but does not worship it. They know that true intelligence includes the consciousness as well as the unseen. Their strategy is informed not only by analysis but also by listening to what moves beneath the surface. They pause before leaping. They sense before they scale. Because of this, their timing is precise therefore making their choices aligned with their results often uncanny.

Together, these four archetypes represent the future of wealth. Not as accumulation, but as integration. Giving extreme light to presence more than performance. Ensuring that harmony is put before hierarchy. They are not personas to be copied but, instead, living blueprints for what is now possible.

These are not roles you play, but they are identities you become through individuation and symbolic wealth reclamation. This is what makes your financial transformation truly revolutionary, not just a personal healing but also as a collective re-patterning. Your individuation becomes a mirror for others. Essentially creating structured clarity out in the financial fields. Your presence rewrites what wealth can mean for an entire generation.

To truly rewire your mind for financial success, you must walk the entire spiral, from personal shadow into archetypal reintegration, and from collective distortion into new cultural symbols. The journey is not linear. It is circular. Wealth, at this level, is no longer about acquisition. It becomes activation. It becomes the field where the psyche evolves in real time, where archetypes are embodied and the future is shaped not just by what we do, but by who we dare to become.

In the new paradigm of wealth, we no longer outsource our fate to broken systems. We make the inner situation conscious. We choose wholeness.

New myths are authored to be lived for liberation rather than for performance. These are archetypes in action. And this is wealth, made conscious.

Among the most potent in shaping your financial life are the archetypes of the anima and animus. The anima and animus are Jung's terms for the unconscious feminine in men and the unconscious masculine in women. Jung taught that every person contains both masculine and feminine psychological energies. The anima, the inner feminine, lives within the psyche of a man. She is the embodiment of feeling, intuition, creativity, and relationship. The animus, the inner masculine, resides within the psyche of a woman. He is the voice of logic, authority, discernment, and direction.

While these archetypes transcend gender identity, they hold massive influence over how we relate to money. When the anima or animus is underdeveloped, your financial decisions become skewed. A man whose anima unconsciously may chase wealth through hyper-rationality dismisses intuition and over-identifies with achievement. His net worth rises, but his fulfillment declines. Another example is that this man may earn, but he cannot receive.

The anima, when ignored, becomes a sabotaging siren, and it can lead to impulsive choices or worse emotional suppression. A man who ignores his anima lives as if one half of his psyche has been exiled. His intuition becomes a stranger, and his inner world a threat. Wealth, in such a state, becomes compensation and a way to fill the void left by emotional disconnection. He builds empires, but not intimacy. This man may accumulate tremendous assets but not have one day of peace.

The repressed anima eventually revolts, not always through catastrophe, but often through quiet dissatisfaction. The man begins to question the very thing he built his life upon. What was all this for? Why does success feel hollow? Why, after acquiring everything, does he still feel unseen? It is at this crossroads that true individuation begins. When the anima is reintegrated and not as a weakness a man regains access to emotional clarity. He begins to sense the tone beneath the numbers, the energy behind the deal, and the alignment behind the opportunity. Financial decisions are no longer just calculations; they become conversations with the soul. Wealth is no longer driven by domination but, instead, by resonance. In this scenario, the man no longer asks, "What will this make me?" but, instead, "What will this cost my truth?" This is not softness at all. This is sovereign masculinity that has made peace with his inner feminine side and, therefore. with his own humanity.

So, what of the woman and her animus? For many women, the animus becomes a battleground. Essentially conditioned to distrust their own authority, many women project their power onto external figures such as mentors or even partners. More often suppressing their inner voice that dares to lead. The undeveloped animus manifests as indecision or even oscillation between overworking and undercharging.

She may possess intuition in abundance, but without the animus to direct it, that intuition becomes silenced in the noise of societal demands. When the animus is integrated, however, the woman becomes sovereign in her decision-making. Her intuition no longer floats ungrounded, and it finds structure. She begins to discern between aligned risk and unconscious reactivity. Her leadership no longer second-guesses her value. Instead, she names her price, not from ego, but from essence. Even more importantly, she honors her inner voice as the final authority. This woman no longer waits for permission to prosper. Instead, she unequivocally becomes the one who grants it.

In both cases, the anima or animus is not domination but, rather, dialogue. Financial sovereignty is born not when one archetype rules but when both dance. The man who integrates his anima does not lose his edge. He refines it. The woman who honors her animus does not become rigid. She becomes clear. This integration is not merely psychological. It is the alchemy of individuation in action.

Jung referred to this process as the inner union that leads to psychic wholeness or a state in which your outer life no longer contradicts your inner truth. In the realm of financial creation, this union is transformational. It marks the shift from unconscious compensation to conscious contribution. You are no longer earning from the wound. You are creating from the whole and this is profound.

When the anima and animus are at war, money becomes the battleground. Every investment, every negotiation, every opportunity is filtered through unconscious distortions: "If I succeed, I will be abandoned," "If I lead, I will be punished," "If I receive, I will be judged." But when these inner archetypes are reconciled and when the anima is no longer rejected, and the animus no longer inflated, your financial life becomes coherent. You begin to choose from a felt sense of alignment rather than from fear. Your income becomes a mirror of your inner order. Your wealth becomes a reflection of your inner peace, and it is visibly felt.

This archetypal reintegration requires symbolic action and somatic practices that invite the unconscious to speak. One may begin by asking: What does my anima want me to feel that I've been avoiding? Where does my animus want me to take a stand I've been postponing? These are the types of starting point questions when an integration is actioned. Please note that these are not surface-level inquiries but are initiations. They invite the psyche to move from stagnation to movement. Dreams, too, become vital during this process. Jung believed that dreams are messages from the unconscious, bearing symbols that can reveal which archetypes are active or repressed.

When you are on the verge of a financial breakthrough or breakdown, then your dreams often shift. Perhaps a recurring image of a crumbling house, a lost child, a golden key, or a closed door emerges. These are not random. They are archetypal signposts. When you interpret your dreams through the lens of individuation, they can show you which parts of your psyche need your attention before your next financial decision. For example, a woman dreaming of losing her voice while standing on stage may be receiving a message from her animus. The dream reveals her unconscious fear of visibility and the unspoken contract she holds that power is dangerous.

If left unexamined, this dream becomes reality. However, if she dialogues with the dream figure through active imagination or symbolic journaling, then she begins to rewire the pattern. She gives voice to the part that was silenced, and in doing so, she reclaims power from within. This is the understanding on how archetypes become allies rather than saboteurs. They do not disappear, but they evolve. They become guides in your financial journey, helping you make decisions that serve the soul, not just the spreadsheet.

When this level of inner alignment is achieved, the external world begins to respond—not because of mystical coincidence, but because your behavior and energy begin to carry clarity. You no longer approach money from desperation, but from discernment. Integrity is not sold for approval, nor does it collapse your voice to keep peace. At this point, you begin to trust the quiet knowing inside you more than the noise outside. And that is what makes wealth sustainable.

In this light, wealth becomes a sacred expression of your individuation. It is a byproduct rather than a goal. A mirror of inner union is formed and not the trophy of ego. When the anima and animus are integrated, when the self is centered, and when the subconscious is no longer filled with shadows, only then does financial success become soulful. It no longer pulls you away from who you are, but instead, it brings you home.

Closing Statement:

To rewire your mind for financial success is to remember what your conditioning made you forget—that wealth is not something you chase but, rather, something you align with. Through individuation, you reclaim your inner authority. Through archetypal integration, you restore the balance between intuition and logic.

In that restoration, wealth begins to reflect coherence. However, there is one layer deeper still, because true wealth does not only test your vision, but it also tests your shadow. It asks, "Can you hold power without losing your center? Can you rise without abandoning the parts of you still afraid of being seen?"

In the next chapter, we'll explore this sacred confrontation with the hidden fears that emerge when power becomes real. What you cannot hold in shadow, you cannot sustain in light. Let us now enter Chapter 10: Wealth, Power, and the Shadow.

CHAPTER TEN

Wealth, Power, and the Shadow: Overcoming Psychological Barriers

"The most terrifying thing is to accept oneself completely."

—*Carl Jung*

Wealth is rarely a matter of numbers. It is, at its core, a reckoning with the parts of the self that we have learned to avoid. That reckoning, in Jungian terms, is known as shadow integration. Most people sabotage their wealth not because they lack talent but because they haven't made peace with the psychological implications of having power. They unconsciously associate wealth with becoming the very thing they fear or were once harmed by: greedy, corrupt, or domineering people.

This fear doesn't arise in the conscious mind. It lives beneath it, in the realm of the shadow. Jung described the shadow as the "thing a person has no wish to be." It contains not only repressed traumas and fears but also disowned gifts and forgotten strengths.

In the context of wealth, this means the shadow often carries the psychological content of power that we were taught to mistrust, power we projected onto others, and power we never learned to wield responsibly. To become successful or even wealthy is not merely to earn more but it is also to confront the deeper question: "Can I handle who I must become to hold more?"

This is where most people stop, not because they are weak, but because wealth threatens to awaken the visionary parts of themselves that they have spent a lifetime trying to exile. The psyche does not resist wealth. It resists the power it would take to embody wealth, and that resistance is sacred. It signals that the self has not yet been prepared to meet the reality it claims to want.

The Shadow Side of Success

Success brings visibility, and visibility brings scrutiny. Then scrutiny triggers the fear of exile.

For centuries, power was reserved for the few, and claiming it without permission was a dangerous act. In many lineages, prosperity was associated with betrayal. In some instances, to be wealthy meant to emulate oppressors.

These legacies don't just live in textbooks, but they live in bone memory. In dreams, defenses, and hesitations we can't explain. When someone steps into success, they aren't just claiming money. They're also confronting inherited fears encoded in their emotional DNA. Suddenly, they're not just dealing with taxes, business models, or visibility, but they're also managing the ghosts of tribal memory. These memories whisper, "If you rise, you'll be alone. If you have more, you'll lose love. If you stand out, you'll be punished."

These aren't just psychological barriers; they are also societal echoes. This is why so many people unconsciously limit their wealth to match their relationships. They fear being "too much"—too free, too bold, and too successful to be loved in the same way.

This is about belonging as opposed to greed. The subconscious would choose to continue to earn less than rather than risk rejection by the tribe. It would comfortably live in quiet struggle than experience the isolation of outgrowing the system that raised it. In this way, the desire for connection overrides the desire for growth, because the inner child fears abandonment more than lack.

In Jungian terms, this is a form of archetypal entanglement. The self is caught between the emerging self and the authentic, individuating core as well as the inherited persona. The persona, Jung explained, is the social mask worn to gain acceptance and identity within a group. It is not inherently negative, but we all need personas to function in society. When a person begins to identify only with that mask and when the persona becomes fused with self-worth, then it turns from a tool into a trap.

Many high achievers unconsciously perform scarcity because their persona depends on it. They perform humility, even martyrdom, because wealth would threaten the image they've curated as "good." This creates an emotional paradox. They desire outward success, but inwardly, it feels dangerous. The closer they get to prosperity, the more their psyche experiences dissonance. The shadow gets louder because they're evolving.

What's often mistaken for self-sabotage is actually self-protection. It's the nervous system doing its best to maintain coherence with an old identity. It says: "If being wealthy will make me lose love; I'll stay broke. If charging more makes me feel selfish, I'll undercharge. If becoming successful means, I betray my roots, then I'll play small and call it integrity."

This isn't laziness or a lack of desire, but it is the grief of becoming someone your old world might not recognize. Inner power requires shedding the persona and not rejecting it entirely but, rather, evolving beyond it. True wealth asks, "Who must I become to be whole?"

Wholeness does not guarantee applause. At times, it will cost you closeness, especially in relationships that were sustained by your self-negation. As you grow, others may see you differently, and that shift can feel like a death to the persona you once wore.

This, too, is part of the shadow journey. Jung understood that any real transformation, and especially one involving power, will require the death of the old self. This is not a physical death. It is a symbolic one. It's a letting go of the masks you used to wear to survive.

That symbolic death is terrifying. It's why many return to the comfort of the known struggle instead of entering the unknown success. However, those who walk through it and who allow the persona to loosen enough so that the true self rises will experience a rebirth that wealth alone could never deliver. They don't just become richer, but they also become real and sovereign.

From there, success no longer feels like exile at all. It feels like embodiment. Here's the paradox: Once you accept the parts of yourself you once exiled, others do too. What you integrate within, you no longer must fight for outside. Your very presence speaks for you, and you become magnetic because of truth rather than because of performance.

This is the shadow side of success. It is not just the fear of failure but also the deeper fear of transformation. It's the knowing that, if you truly claim your wealth and your power, you can never unsee what you've seen. This is when power is no longer a performance but, instead, is a quiet, steady presence. This means to no longer abandon yourself. It doesn't mean to dominate others. When the shadow softens, the success and wealth become real.

Power As Shadow; Power As Potential

In Jung's work, power was never viewed as inherently evil. Instead, what made power dangerous was its unconsciousness. When we project power onto others or onto institutions then we disown our ability to self-author. We become passive, even if we are externally successful. Jung referred to this as a loss of center, where the ego becomes subject to collective forces because it has not anchored in its own sovereignty.

To reclaim your financial power, then, is not just about affirmations or assertiveness. It is also about returning to center. Returning to center, in Jungian language, is the self and not the ego. The self is the totality of the psyche. It is the organizing principle that seeks wholeness. It contains both light and shadow. It doesn't choose sides, but it includes and witnesses. To approach wealth from this place is to make peace with the paradoxes of being human. You can be wealthy and generous. You can be powerful and kind as well as influential yet humble.

These are not contradictions. They are integrations that can only arise through the confrontation of the shadow not by transcending it, but by transforming it. This confrontation can take many forms. For example, it may be a failed business, a betrayal, a financial loss, or a public humiliation.

These events are not random at all, but they are rites. The psyche uses them as symbolic moments to initiate you into your next level of authorship. They arrive when the old identity can no longer carry the weight of your becoming. They ask: Can you hold power without losing yourself? Can you receive more without abandoning your integrity?

Can you become visible without shrinking or inflating?

In the modern world, we learn to pursue the benefits of influence without understanding how to build the inner structure required to carry them. So, when power by way of influence finally arrives, it often cracks the identity. Without conscious integration, success activates the very wounds it was meant to soothe.

A child who was ignored may use wealth to finally feel seen, but without shadow work, that need becomes insatiable. A person who was betrayed may use success to feel safe, but without healing, that fear turns into hyper-control. What was meant to liberate becomes another form of enslavement.

Jung warned that the shadow, when unintegrated, will always be projected outward. You will see in others what you refuse to see in yourself. When it comes to money, that projection is often ferocious. You will hate the wealthy because you are afraid to become them. You will resent the successful because a part of you has not yet claimed your own potential. You will distrust leadership because your inner authority is still dormant. The bitterness isn't random. It is instructive, and it tells you where power has not yet been integrated within.

What we demonize externally is often the aspect of power we've refused to honor within. And yet, paradoxically, that refusal gives it more control. When you exile your own potential, it doesn't disappear. It just goes underground. It becomes distorted, surfacing through sabotage or paralysis. The parts of you that could lead begin to turn against you because they are unclaimed rather than bad.

The solution is not to avoid power. It's to redefine power. In Jungian terms, power is not force. It is presence, and it is congruence rather than control. Real power does not posture or dominate. Real power aligns, and it does not need to convince because it resonates.

This is the difference between egoic ambition and archetypal presence. One grasps while the other attracts. When you begin to hold power from the self, not the persona, a subtle shift takes place. You no longer need to perform. You become more grounded, less reactive, and more attuned. The decisions you make whether about money, leadership, visibility, or investment then begin to reflect your wholeness and not your wound. Wealth becomes less about what you own and more about what you embody.

This reclamation of power is not a one-time event. It is a spiral, with each level of success summoning a new layer of shadow. Each elevation will test the nervous system, the identity, and the intention behind your ambitions. This is where power becomes more than just something you claim. It becomes something you are entrusted with.

Jung often taught that true power is not about holding on. It is about holding space—holding your truth when it's unpopular and holding your vision when it's doubted. This is not easy work, especially in a world where power is so often abused. In this context, the integration of the shadow becomes an act of collective healing. Every person who reclaims power from the unconscious elevates the culture. Every leader who operates from the self instead of the wound becomes a template for transformation.

Redefining Power Through Inner Integration

Jung taught that the path to wholeness is never straight. It is a spiral of symbols, patterns, and returning truths. Each encounter with the shadow is a rite of passage, not a detour.

Nowhere is this more evident than in our relationship to power and wealth. For most people, power has been conflated with control. But, in its truest form, power is not about control at all. It is about presence. True power is the capacity to remain fully conscious in the face of discomfort. It's the ability to stay rooted when your nervous system wants to flee. It's the willingness to tell the truth even when it costs you approval, and to lead from an inner resonance with integrity.

When applied to wealth, this reframes everything. Wealth is no longer a mask for insecurity nor a stage for performance. It becomes a reflection of inner congruence, and that congruence can only emerge when we stop running from the shadow. That is because the real psychological barrier to wealth is not lack of strategy; it is the internal fragmentation that keeps power and vulnerability at war within us.

To become sovereign is to end that war. In Jungian terms, the mature ego is not inflated by power nor paralyzed by doubt. The mature ego bows to the self, the organizing force of the psyche that contains both light and shadow. This bow is not submission. It is alignment. It is the beginning of a new relationship with money that is relational instead of rigid. You can receive without guilt, charge what you're worth without apology, and make bold decisions without dissociating from your body.

This is the work behind the work and, while it doesn't sparkle like vision boards or polished high-performance routines, it delivers something far greater than surface-level success: capacity. This is the capacity to hold more wealth without collapsing, to lead without projecting, and to be visible without losing your center.

Shadow work is rarely glamorous, yet it is the doorway to a kind of psychological power that cannot be taken from you, it can only be earned through integration. Jung reminded us that the shadow grows stronger the longer it is left unattended. So, when you find yourself caught in cycles of sabotage, stalled growth, or unease in the presence of abundance, this is not evidence of failure. It is the psyche's way of drawing you inward, inviting you to evolve rather than collapse into shame. In truth, your unconscious is trying to reveal the inherited stories and hidden contracts that have shaped how you relate to power, prosperity, and visibility. And within this deeper encounter lies the realization that the next stage of your wealth is not achieved by doing more, but by becoming more whole.

Because the final truth is this: unintegrated power always becomes projection, but integrated power becomes peace. When you move through the world from peace, wealth follows not as compensation for your wounds but as a reflection of your coherence.

Liberating Wealth From the Shadow: The Final Threshold

Every psychological barrier to wealth is, at its core, a fragmentation of the self. It is a part of you that learned through trauma or circumstance that wealth could not be trusted and seen as safe. These beliefs do not live on the surface of your mind. They are buried deep in your body's memory, in your nervous system, and in the symbolic language of your unconscious. The beliefs appear as hesitation or the inability to hold what you've created.

The good news is these barriers are not fixed. They are thresholds, and every threshold is an invitation to initiate a new relationship with power. Overcoming these psychological barriers is not about fixing yourself. It's about meeting yourself where the fear lives and doing so with curiosity instead of judgment. It's about asking: Which part of me is afraid to expand? Who am I protecting by staying small? What loyalty am I unconsciously honoring by staying underpaid, unseen, or under-resourced?

Most people try to override these patterns with productivity and many times by over performance. Yet the psyche cannot be bypassed, and it must be heard as well as felt. The only way through resistance is intimacy and to ask it what it needs.

When you do this, you begin to unfreeze the parts of you that learned to associate wealth with danger. You create inner safety not by repressing the shadow but by bringing it into the conversation. You become the adult presence your inner child was waiting for. You become the sovereign self who can finally rewrite the script.

Jung believed that real freedom comes not from disowning the unconscious but from integrating it. In the realm of wealth, this means choosing to become aware of every time you collapse your power to maintain comfort. Every time you reject abundance to stay connected. Every time you pretend to be less than you are to avoid disrupting the equilibrium of your environment.

Freedom begins when you stop outsourcing your worth. This is the moment when wealth becomes more than numbers, and it becomes a narrative. You are no longer repeating your past but authoring your future. You are no longer waiting for permission to prosper. Instead, you are becoming the source of it.

Overcoming psychological barriers to wealth is not a single act. It is a lifelong spiral of remembering the exiled parts of yourself, reclaiming the symbols you were taught to fear, and rewriting the roles you were told to play in order to transmute. From this transmutation, a new financial reality begins to emerge that is shaped by the full presence of your sovereign, integrated self.

Closing Statement:

In the end, power is not something you seize. It is something you remember. Beneath every psychological barrier to wealth lies a forgotten truth, an unintegrated part of the self-waiting to return home. The shadow is not your enemy; it is your guide. It does not block abundance. It guards the threshold until you are ready to hold it without self-abandonment.

To overcome the inner resistance to wealth is to reclaim what you once disowned: your voice, your value, and your authority. This is not about becoming more. It is about becoming whole, and wholeness is the most magnetic force in the universe.

Wealth, at its highest expression, is not a reward. It is a reflection that mirrors back to you the frequency you hold, the truths you embody, and the power you have reclaimed. As you step forward into the next chapter, remember that what you attract is not determined by how loudly you chase but by how clearly you resonate. Wealth does not arrive through force; it arrives through frequency.

CHAPTER ELEVEN

Wealth Attraction Through Energy and Frequency

"The psyche is not of today; its ancestry goes back many millions of years. Individual consciousness is only the flower and the fruit of a season, sprung from the perennial rhizome beneath the earth."
—*Carl Jung*

There is a moment on the wealth journey when logic grows quiet. The spreadsheets, systems, and step-by-step strategies fade into the background, and something subtler begins to lead. It might start as a pull or a ripple of knowing that isn't quite explainable but insists on being followed. In the old paradigm, this is where many turn back, clutching their rational mind like a compass. Yet, in the new wealth paradigm—the one rooted in wholeness and sovereignty—this is where the real journey begins, toward energetic coherence and the terrain of frequency instead of away from the truth.

Wealth, in this realm, is not only earned but it is attuned to. It is not only pursued but it is received. To attract wealth through energy and frequency is not to abandon action but, rather, to align it. It is to make your presence so vibrationally precise that the outer world has no choice but to reflect your inner state. We are now entering a chapter that requires a different kind of intelligence and one that Jung knew well, but the modern financial world often forgets. It is the intelligence of resonance, or the invisible architecture of the psyche and its interaction with the field we call reality.

Jung never used the language of "vibrations" or "frequency" in the modern spiritual sense, but he came remarkably close. In his work on synchronicity, dreams, and the nature of the collective unconscious, Jung was constantly circling the mystery of energetic causality and the idea that reality is shaped not only by physical forces, but by psychological and symbolic ones.

In this sense, your psyche is not just a container for thoughts, but it is also a transmitter. It is a frequency field that is constantly attracting, interpreting, and shaping experience. Jung compared this activity to fantasy, not as idle imagination, but as the mechanism through which the psyche continuously brings inner meaning into the world. It is this creative energetic field that underlies how we attract and shape our external experience.

In other words, your inner frequency determines what outer patterns appear. When you are aligned, life speaks clearly, and when you are fragmented, life reflects distortion. The collective misunderstanding is that most people attempt to shift their outer reality without first recalibrating their energetic signal. They treat money as math, forgetting that beneath every number is a narrative, and beneath every narrative is a frequency.

So, what is frequency mastery in the context of wealth? It is the art of becoming the kind of person that wealth trusts—not because you said the right affirmation, but because your field is clean, and your intentions are coherently exhibiting energetic truth.

Energetic truth is about allowing your entire being as well as your thoughts, emotions, and archetypal patterns to come into an integrated coherence. In the Jungian sense, this means the ego does not try to override the unconscious with force. Instead, the ego collaborates with the unconscious through attunement. True frequency mastery begins when your conscious and unconscious intentions align, creating a field of resonance strong enough to magnetize new outcomes. This is where wealth attraction becomes not an act of force but of presence. You don't need to chase the thing you are already becoming. You don't need to convince the universe you're ready.

When your energy is clean, the results reflect that clarity. The work then becomes one of inner stewardship: managing your signal, not your circumstances; making sure that your nervous system can support expansion; and making sure that the part of you who wants to receive is not in battle with the part of you who feels undeserving. This, Jung might say, is when the transcendent function begins to operate.

The Transcendent Function: Bridging the Seen and the Unseen

Jung introduced the concept of the transcendent function as the inner mechanism that reconciles opposites and brings them into a new synthesis. Rather than forcing a choice between the conscious and the unconscious, or between reason and feeling, it creates a third path that holds both. In the realm of wealth and frequency, this function becomes an energetic bridge. It takes the tension between fear and possibility, between old patterns and new visions, and transforms that friction into a coherent signal capable of carrying you into higher resonance.

Most people approach money from an internal dichotomy. One part of them wants wealth while another fears what wealth will bring. One part wants to be seen while another is terrified of judgment. One part trusts the psyche while another clings to control. These internal divisions create a fragmented frequency that must be coherent to carry power. To work with the transcendent function is to allow the psyche to do its inner weaving. This is not passive. It requires holding the tension of opposites without collapsing into one side or the other.

You must learn to hold the desire to expand and the fear of change in the same breath, without forcing resolution. From that tension, something new emerges. It is not an intellectual solution but, rather, an energetic integration. This integration shifts your field, and you will start to notice that you no longer sabotage opportunities, that conversations flow, and that timing aligns.

This is not coincidence at all. It is the frequency of inner wholeness expressing itself in outer reality. Jung knew this truth long before energy language became mainstream: wholeness is magnetic. One of the most overlooked aspects of energetic wealth attraction is what could be called psyche entanglement. This is when our energy becomes enmeshed with people, beliefs, or identities that distort our signal. Jung would describe this as participation mystique, a phenomenon where individuals unconsciously merge their identity with others, often sacrificing autonomy in the process.

In family systems, this might show up as unconscious loyalty to financial struggle. In romantic dynamics, it may manifest as guilt for outearning a partner. In business, it can appear as people-pleasing clients at the expense of your own value. Energetic entanglement weakens the frequency field. It creates leaks that will make you work twice as hard for half the results, not because you lack skill but because your frequency is distorted.

Reclaiming your wealth frequency, then, requires disentangling—not from people, per se, but from projections that no longer serve your expansion. This process often requires deep inner witnessing; noticing where guilt or obligation speaks louder than clarity; and knowing when you have internalized a certain archetype role. When these energetic threads are cleared, something remarkable happens: the external world reorganizes. Clients respond differently, and opportunities emerge without strain. Conversations shift tone. You are no longer relating to money through the residue of old entanglements. Instead, you are relating to it through your individuated, sovereign signal.

Symbolic Wealth and the Archetypal Field

Throughout my investigation, one truth has echoed louder than all others. Every culture encodes money with symbolic meaning.

For some, wealth is a symbol of safety. For others, it conjures images of betrayal, corruption, or power imbalances. These meanings are not merely personal. They are archetypal. Each of us walks through life within this symbolic architecture, often unaware of how deeply it shapes our relationship with wealth. To work with energy is to work with these symbols. To shift frequency is not just to "feel better" but, also, to become conscious of what money truly symbolizes in your inner world.

Ask yourself: What did money represent to my inner child? What did it mean in my family system? Did it mean conflict, abandonment, and control? Or was it tied to freedom, joy, or validation? These symbolic patterns live beneath every financial decision. If, in your unconscious field, money represents danger, domination, or exile, your conscious desire for abundance will always meet resistance. Frequency becomes fragmented and attraction becomes erratic.

This is why people can spend decades pursuing wealth but never feel secure in it. The inner symbol remains unhealed. Jung would remind us that symbols are not fixed. They are living, they evolve, and they can be reclaimed. Through active imagination or dreamwork we can re-author what money means to us. We can take it out of the hands of fear, and infuse it with the energy of service and creativity.

When this shift occurs, money is no longer an external force we chase or fear. It becomes a relational field and a mirror of our inner coherence. At this level, wealth becomes symbolic authorship. You are no longer bound to the mythologies of your culture or lineage. You assign meaning to your frequency shifts from re-alignment instead of force.

But let me be clear: frequency mastery is not a one-time breakthrough. It requires devotion and commitment. High-frequency living is not accidental but intentional. It is a recalibration of your field every single day. It requires you to return to coherence. Every morning becomes an opportunity to choose truth over performance, alignment over autopilot, and inner clarity over external noise.

Jung often emphasized that the psyche's evolution is a lifelong process, and the same is true for the energy of wealth. Your financial field must grow alongside your inner development. As your values deepen and shift, the structures that hold your wealth must adjust to reflect your new frequency. What once felt aligned may naturally fall away, making space for a higher, more coherent resonance.

Frequency does not cling. It flows, and so must you. This is where wealth leadership truly begins. High-frequency leadership doesn't mean bypassing fear. It means noticing it without obeying it. This would require checking in with your nervous system before a business decision. It means ending a client relationship not because it failed, but because it no longer reflects your truth. This is the sacred discipline of wealth re-patterning.

Jung believed that the psyche evolves in spirals and not straight lines. Our growth is symbolic and often circular. That means your financial patterns will return—but as invitation rather than as a punishment. Each time you see a pattern, you have the chance to meet it differently. You have the opportunity to choose presence over panic, intuition over impulse, and self-trust over sabotage.

Every time you do, you code a new frequency into your field. This is not about repeating affirmations. This is about embodied repetition. There is a difference. It's about living the new frequency, especially when it's difficult. This is true especially when old patterns beg to be repeated, because it is in these moments that your frequency either anchors or unravels. This is why most people plateau. It is not because they're lazy but because they confuse breakthrough with completion.

I have learned that frequency is not a destination. It is a rhythm that must be tuned. Like a fine instrument, your energetic field needs constant harmonizing not because it's broken but because it is alive.

When you live at this level of integrity, your outer world shifts. Opportunities begin to match your essence. Money flows with less effort, and decisions feel more intuitive. Your abundance becomes less about what you do and more about who you are being.

Jung once said, "The outer situation is only ever the reflection of an inner condition." Change the inner condition, and the outer reality responds. This is the essence of wealth attraction through energy and frequency. It's not through magical thinking but, instead, because of psychological precision. It's not surface performance. It is symbolic embodiment.

In sacred alignment, your wealth becomes more than material. It becomes mythic—a living symbol of your inner transformation and a reflection of your psyche's coherence.

Closing Statement:

To attract wealth through energy and frequency is not to escape the material world. It is to animate it with meaning. It is to remember that what you earn is inseparable from who you become.

Wealth is not separate from your inner life. It is a mirror and a living conversation between your psyche and the world. Frequency mastery is not spiritual theater. It is the courageous, continuous practice of inner coherence. It is choosing to align your nervous system, your decisions, your symbols, and your soul until reality has no choice but to meet you where you truly are.

This is when wealth no longer arrives as a reward but as recognition. The future of wealth is encoded in presence, felt in resonance, and built through the frequency of integrity. So let your wealth journey be one of energetic maturity and precision, because the more whole you become, the more inevitable your abundance becomes.

CHAPTER TWELVE

Archetypal Analysis of Wealthy Individuals

"A man who has not passed through the inferno of his passions has never overcome them."
—*Carl Jung*

We've journeyed past the surface of formulas, charts, and affirmations to explore the deeper architecture of the psyche, arriving in a space where wealth is experienced as sovereignty and energy flows in alignment with our inner truth. This is a realm of transformation that touches the depths of who we are, not just what we achieve. It is here that we turn our attention to the lives of those who have navigated this terrain on a grand scale, whose stories reflect the principles of conscious wealth and psychological mastery.

The purpose is not to idolize but, instead, to investigate and ask, what do modern billionaires reveal about archetypes in action? What lessons arise when psychological sovereignty meets mega success?

Let's examine two individuals whose public lives and documented narratives offer us insight: Warren Buffett, and Oprah Winfrey. Each reflects an archetypal matrix in which personal shadow and collective myth intersect, shaped by their own individuation path and the archetypes they animate.

Warren Buffett: The Sage Investor

Warren Buffett's billion-dollar discipline, value investing and patience all embody the archetype of the sage. His strategy is not impulsive or flashy. It is grounded in clarity and deep reflection. Buffett's lifetime partnership with Charlie Munger illustrates his commitment to humble wisdom, probability thinking, and ethical steadiness. Jungians might recognize in Buffett the "Wise Man" archetype, which is an embodiment of inner consonance, non-reactive knowing, and right-timed action.

Even his unremarkable lifestyle includes a modest home and simple pleasures, and signals a grounding in self, not persona. Buffett's shadow emerges not in scandal or hubris, but in what he admits: a bias toward inaction, skepticism of innovation, and occasional detachment from the emotional element of investing. His stoic approach tethers him to safety; his legend shows that authority is only sustained when integrated with humility and adaptability.

Buffett teaches us that enduring wealth is not built in bursts of brilliance but in seasons of discipline. His success is not the result of extraordinary risks or revolutionary breakthroughs but of extraordinary consistency.

In a world that idolizes speed, Buffett reminds us that sovereignty often looks like stillness. We learn that the truest power is not reactive but reflective, and that wealth responds to alignment rather than anxiety.

Buffett's approach shows us that prosperity grows when the ego steps aside and the inner sage is allowed to lead. The sage archetype teaches us to trust the slow burn of knowledge, to wait for right timing, and to act only when our values and data are both in agreement. We also learn that emotional regulation is a form of wealth stewardship. Buffett has trained himself to remain calm amid chaos, to delay gratification when the world panics, and to remember that every financial decision is a vote for one's long-term self. This psychological mastery over urgency and market hype is rare and deeply teachable. Buffett's legacy is not only his portfolio; it's his presence. He models that it is possible to be powerful and humble. In this, he stands as a living archetype of integrated power and a reminder that success is not about dominating the world but about mastering yourself within it. So, when we study Warren Buffett, we are not merely studying investment strategy. We are also studying the psychological infrastructure of sustained abundance. We are learning how to build wealth that lasts because it is not built on performance but, rather, on principle.

In the new wealth paradigm, Buffett reminds us that you don't need to be flashy to be free. You don't need to chase trends to be trusted. What you need is clarity and integrity. Most importantly, you need the courage to live in alignment with what you know to be true even when the world doubts it. That is the frequency of the sage and the real secret behind the billions.

Oprah Winfrey: The Empowered Healer Archetype

Oprah Winfrey's life narrative reflects profound depth and evolution. Rising from poverty and trauma, she built an empire rooted in stories and the human heart. This aligns her with the healer archetype, someone who transforms suffering into resonance and compassion while catalyzing others' healing.

Her story is extraordinary. She is the orphan who becomes queen of influence, then turns her wealth outward to support education and empowerment.

Jung noted that the healer may become wounded by success, but those wounds may also become the source of authenticity and connection. Oprah's transparency about her vulnerabilities during interviews in which she shares her own battles signals exactly such integration.

Her shadow can show up as over-identification with public persona. Her voice must balance the gift of empathy with autonomy. Still, her sustained alignment with her inner self and her commitment to learning through mentors like Maya Angelou demonstrates that real power inheres not in acclaim, but in self-authoring intactness.

So, what can we learn? Oprah teaches us that true wealth is relational before it is transactional. She shows that power becomes magnetic when it is rooted in emotional congruence and when your outer life reflects the truth of your inner world. She teaches us that vulnerability is not a liability. It is leadership.

In a culture that equates success with stoicism, Oprah reminds us that softness and empathy are not the opposite of wealth. They are the soil it grows in. Her career proves that, when your voice is attuned to the emotional landscape of the collective, your work becomes timeless.

Oprah's path exemplifies the transformative power of symbolic redefinition. She took forces that might have once constrained her like her gender or her early trauma and transmuted them into emblems of influence. In doing so, she demonstrates one of the highest forms of wealth creation: turning inherited pain into a force that empowers not only herself but the collective.

She also teaches us about the importance of sacred boundaries. Even the most loving leaders must learn where they end and others begin. Through her life and choices, we learn that autonomy is unselfish and sacred. We discover, that the gift of holding space for others must be matched with the discipline of returning to oneself.

Perhaps most importantly, Oprah embodies the lesson that your story is your sovereignty. When your narrative becomes a vessel of service, and when your truth becomes your transmission, wealth is not just something you build. It is also something you become.

Her legacy is a call to wholeness: to tell the truth even when it trembles, to walk forward even when uninvited, and to lead not from perfection, but from presence. Oprah's life is a testament that authority does not require loudness, that sovereign wealth grows when your inner story blesses what you build, and that leadership becomes poetic when it contains vulnerability.

She reminds us that you don't need to inherit power to generate it. You only need the courage to alchemize your story, trust your intuition, and honor the field your presence creates. In a world obsessed with what people own, Oprah teaches us to look at what people embody. And that, perhaps, is the greatest wealth of all.

Weaving the Archetypal Code: A Psychological Synthesis of Wealth

When viewed through a symbolic and Jungian lens, the lives of Warren Buffett and Oprah Winfrey reflect two profound psychological truths: that wealth, in its truest form, is an extension of individuation, and that mastery of external power must first arise from inner integration.

These figures are not simply billionaires by economic standards; they are embodiments of archetypal resonance. They have become who they truly are, and the world has responded accordingly.

Warren Buffett stands as the archetype of the sage and his life governed by reflective pause and ethical fortitude. His wealth is not reactionary but emergent, cultivated from psychological spaciousness rather than strategic speed. He demonstrates the fact that long-term abundance is rarely born from urgency. It's born from inner coherence.

In Buffett's stillness, we see a wealth that listens before it acts. In his restraint, we see the power of containment and a refusal to be seduced by noise. Jung taught that the wise man archetype carries the light of wisdom and inner direction. Buffett's empire was constructed not through force, but through fidelity to his internal compass.

On the other hand, Oprah Winfrey reveals the path of the sovereign healer. Her voice carries the energy of the Queen who has known suffering, who has transmuted it, and who now uses her throne to bless others. Her wealth emerged not from avoidance of pain but from integration of it. She shows that psychological congruence, or the place where your public life reflects your private wholeness, is a magnet for sustained success. Whereas Buffett anchors the sage's clarity, Oprah invokes the healer's alchemy.

Both teach us that power without presence is noise, but power with presence is transmission. And here's the most important lesson: these archetypes are not exclusive to billionaires. They are symbolic potentials within each of us.

Jung believed that every human being contains the seeds of every archetype. The question is not whether we have access to these energies, but whether we are willing to confront what stands between us and their full expression.

When we analyze wealth psychology through these archetypal lenses, we begin to decode the deeper message that wealth is not just a number; it is a narrative. It is not just a currency of commerce, but it is a currency of consciousness. It reflects what the psyche believes to be safe.

The sage teaches discernment. The healer teaches resonance, and both reveal that integration is what creates lasting success. This is where many individuals struggle. It is not because they lack intelligence or ambition, but because they are out of sync with their own internal myth. They are chasing a life their psyche has not yet agreed to hold. Jung would say they are still entangled in a persona or complex that has not yet been brought into consciousness.

This is why understanding wealth from a symbolic and psychological lens matters. If your internal story still sees money as dangerous or corrupting, no outer strategy will ever feel safe. If you have not made peace with your own power, you will continue to sabotage or shrink when abundance arrives. But when you begin to live in harmony with your inner archetypes, your frequency shifts and wealth, like a tuning fork, responds.

So, what can we learn? We learn that wealth, in its deepest expression, is psychological sovereignty. It is not about how much you earn but, instead, how fully your actions align with yourself. We learn that leadership is not about domination but about embodiment.

That the richest among us often succeed not because they are flawless, but because they have learned to reconcile their contradictions. They lead from the self and not from the inflated ego, nor the fearful child, but from the integrated whole.

Perhaps the most important lesson to come from my research is that you are not meant to copy another's archetypal blueprint. You are meant to discern your own.

You are not here to replicate Oprah's empathy or Buffett's discipline. You are here to excavate the archetypes already stirring in your unconscious and give them permission to lead.

So, this chapter does not end with a call to mimic but, rather, a call to awaken; to look at the billionaires not as untouchable icons, but as symbolic mirrors; and to see in their paths a map of what is possible when the self is allowed to guide. Their stories teach us that wealth is not reserved for the elite but, rather, it is reserved for the integrated.

CHAPTER THIRTEEN

The Archetypal Wealth Integration Model

Living Wealth as a Daily Practice of Self-Realization: Becoming What You Choose to Be

"The privilege of a lifetime is to become who you truly are."

—Carl Jung

We've journeyed far, moving through the landscapes of symbols and stories, exploring the shadows that shape us, and tracing the paths of sovereign identity. We've encountered timeless archetypes and observed the inner architecture of those who have scaled wealth at extraordinary levels.

But now we arrive at the threshold that truly matters. This is the point where knowledge must become embodiment, and insight must become integration. This chapter is your invitation to cross that threshold. You've seen wealth from every angle: through myth, psyche, energy, and behavior. But unless that insight takes root in your life, it remains abstract. Unless you begin to feel, act, and lead from this deeper knowing, the code remains locked. This chapter is about unlocking it.

We are now going to walk through a five-phase integration process that draws directly from Jung's concept of individuation and the gradual unfolding of the true self as well as the wealth psychologies we've developed in this book. You will not be given a checklist or formula. You will be given a process. One that meets you where you are and evolves with who you are becoming.

Phase 1: Archetypal Recognition – "Name the Pattern"

You cannot transform what you haven't yet named. This is the first and most courageous step. To look within and ask, what archetype is currently driving my financial life? Are you the orphan, waiting to be saved? The martyr, earning love through sacrifice? Or The ruler, craving control?

Jung said the first act of transformation is recognition and, before integration can occur, the unconscious must be made conscious. This phase is about radical honesty, not judgment. It's where you sit with yourself and trace the repeating loops of scarcity, over-giving or avoidance—not to blame but to reveal. When you name the pattern, you loosen its grip. When you identify the archetype, you begin to reclaim choice.

Try this: Write the story of your financial life through the eyes of an archetype. Who shows up most often when you make money decisions? Let them speak and be seen. Remember that this is not performance. It is initiation.

Phase 2: Shadow Excavation – "Face the Resistance"

The part of you that fears power must become a part of the you that learns to hold it. Once you've recognized the archetypal patterns, the next step is to meet the shadow behind them. Shadow work is not a detour; it is the path. Because your shadow holds the keys to your frequency and until it is seen, it runs the show.

This is where you gently ask: What is the emotional root of my money behavior? Where do I carry shame around earning? Who taught me that wealth was dangerous or corrupting? Whose fears have I inherited? Which unconscious contracts still govern my relationship with success?

Use body-based inquiry here. Your nervous system knows, and scarcity often lives in the chest. Shame settles in the gut, and a feeling of "not enoughness" may tighten the throat. You're not here to fight these sensations. You're here to listen to them.

Try this: Map out your money memories across your family line. What roles did your parents, grandparents, or cultural models play? Were they controllers, survivors, or spenders? What myths about wealth were passed down, or were either spoken or unspoken? And, most importantly, do those myths belong to you anymore? To individuate is to choose the myth you now live by.

Phase 3: Frequency Realignment— "Feel the Truth"

You don't attract what you want. You attract what your nervous system believes is safe to hold. This is the phase where awareness begins to move into embodiment. You've uncovered the symbolic code and contacted the shadow. Now you must build the internal safety to hold more wealth and prosperity without defaulting into collapse or sabotage.

Jung's transcendent function offers a powerful model here. It teaches us to hold the tension between opposing forces regarding lack and abundance—for example, fear and desire—without prematurely resolving it. That tension becomes alchemy, and it is not about forcing positivity. It's about becoming present enough to your current emotional reality that the field begins to shift. Frequency work is not mystical fluff. It is biological precision. Your nervous system must feel safe to receive and retain.

Try this: Begin each morning with an "energy calibration" practice. Close your eyes, and anchor into your breath. Ask, "What is my true frequency today?" Don't fake abundance but, instead, tune into it honestly. Use a symbolic mantra to align your system. For example, you might say: "It is safe to be seen" or "I am the frequency of wholeness." Track synchronicities as feedback, not flukes. Your outer world is beginning to reflect your inner coherence.

Phase 4: Sovereign Action— "Move as the Integrated Self"

At this point in your transformation, you're no longer moving from reaction or compensation. You're acting from the self, and this is where you begin to make wealth decisions—not to prove but to express alignment.

In Jungian terms, this is individuation in motion. Your inner masculine and feminine energies (anima/animus) begin to harmonize. You don't hustle blindly or wait passively. Instead, you act with clarity, rhythm, and intuitive attunement. Your investments, partnerships, and expressions begin to match your inner authority.

Try this: Before every major money decision, ask yourself, "Am I acting from my persona or myself?" Let the sacred merchant make your business decisions or the embodied oracle choose your timing. Let the sovereign set your boundaries or the integrated architect build your systems. Every action becomes symbolic when it's rooted in identity. This is not surface level "alignment." it is structural coherence.

Phase 5: Collective Contribution— "Seed the New System"

The ultimate wealth is not ownership; it is symbolic authorship. Once your internal world becomes integrated, your outer world becomes a transmission. The world feels it, and you don't need to force influence, for it flows through you. You become a cultural node of transformation, and this is where wealth begins to expand beyond self-interest into soul-impact.

Jung believed that individuation does not end in isolation. It ends in contribution. The self, once realized, becomes a vessel through which the archetypal field evolves. Wealth, then, is no longer personal. It becomes a way to midwife the mythic shift.

Try this: Craft your legacy symbol or projects that encode your truth into culture. This could be a podcast, a foundation, a teaching, or even a family value system. It doesn't need to be grandiose. It just needs to be real. Ask: If my wealth became a mirror of my deepest values, what would it build? Then build it.

Bringing It All Together: The Archetypal Wealth Integration Analysis

You've now moved through the five phases of transformation with recognition, excavation, realignment, sovereign action, and contribution. But transformation doesn't live in fragments. It reveals itself when the parts converge. In this section, we bring the phases together into a unified lens. This is what I call your Archetypal Wealth Integration Analysis. This is not just a reflection tool. It is also a mirror. Each phase revealed something different.

This journey began in phase one, where you were guided to name your patterns and financial identities, bringing clarity to the unconscious scripts that shaped your relationship with money. In phase two, you unearthed the deeper layers of subconscious resistance and generational burdens, exposing the hidden forces that silently governed your financial behavior. Phase three invited you to recalibrate your nervous system and emotional frequency, creating an internal environment aligned with expansion and worthiness. Then, in phase four, you activated aligned action rooted in sovereignty so that you were no longer reacting from fear but choosing from inner authority. Finally, phase five called you into contribution, asking you to become a living symbol of a new wealth system—one that is conscious, integrated, and rooted in purpose.

But what happens when you step back and analyze the full arc? You begin to see the archetypal blueprint of your personal wealth story. This is where symbolic psychology becomes practical revelation.

To integrate your wealth journey, begin by identifying the dominant wealth archetype shaping your financial behaviors. Perhaps it's the Orphan, who unconsciously avoids stepping into power due to a lingering fear of abandonment or the Martyr, who finds a sense of worth in over-giving, often at their own expense.

These archetypes represent more than behavior. They are also energetic patterns that have quietly shaped your financial reality. Once you name the archetype, the next step is to trace the root of resistance.

Ask yourself: What core fear is this archetype protecting me from? For the Orphan, it may be the fear of being left unsupported; for the Martyr, it may be a belief that receiving diminishes your value.

This tension is your wealth complex, or a psychic knot formed where identity and survival strategies intersect. However, this knot is a key rather than a flaw.

The very pattern that once bound you can become the gateway to your freedom. As awareness deepens, return to the energetic state you accessed when your nervous system felt regulated and safe.

That frequency is your magnetic signature. It isn't temporary; it's a resonance that, when named and nurtured, draws in wealth that feels true to who you really are. Ask yourself: What does wealth feel like when I'm fully aligned with myself?

From here, define your sovereign success archetype or the integrated version of yourself who makes financial decisions from clarity and not compulsion. This archetype isn't a role to chase. It's who you become when you're aligned in action.

Then, reflect on your greater mission. What symbol, service, or vision began to form when you think about contribution? This is more than legacy. It's your personal portal to wealth expansion. Ask: What am I here to restore through my success? What story do I rewrite by simply embodying truth? Because the very parts of you that once felt like flaws or your pain, doubt, or shame are the sacred materials of your transformation.

To bring it all together, create your wealth integration map. It is a five-phase circle of your journey and your core archetype, the shadow you faced, the frequency you now hold, the actions you embodied, and the contribution you feel called to make.

Connect the pieces and watch a new pattern emerge. Give it a name if it feels right to you such as, "The Healer's Legacy" or "The Sovereign Path." Let it be your mirror because, in the end, wealth isn't something you chase, it is something you embody. So, when integration occurs, prosperity becomes a reflection of who you truly are.

Closing Statement:

In a world overflowing with strategies, formulas, and external noise, the most powerful wealth code was never something you had to chase. It was always etched within your psyche, waiting to be reawakened.

Wealth is not merely the result of clever moves or perfect timing. True wealth is the organic result of symbolic alignment and when your values, archetypes, energy, and decisions begin to resonate as one coherent field. You don't just earn, you evolve.

Jung once said, "We are not what happened to us. We are what we choose to become." Let this chapter be your turning point, and let your next decision carry intention. Lastly, let your path no longer be inherited but, instead, be authored.

CHAPTER FOURTEEN

Living the Success Archetype

This final chapter is not simply a recap of ideas; it is a homecoming. It is a return to the destination that this journey has quietly guided us toward all along: a self that is fully awake, sovereign, and complete. We began with a question that underlies every financial choice: What truly creates wealth? Not fleeting success or momentary wins, but the kind of enduring abundance that withstands both external upheaval and internal turbulence.

To answer that, we ventured inward. We entered the terrain of the unconscious, followed the threads of archetypes, confronted shadows, and decoded synchronicities. Along the way, what we discovered wasn't a formula. It was transformation that reconfigures your very identity.

In this model, wealth is not a destination but, rather, it is a mirror of inner coherence. True prosperity only emerges when you stop fragmenting your psyche and begin living from wholeness. Through the lens of Jung's teachings, we've explored how individuation or the journey to the self is not a spiritual theory but, instead, the psychological backbone of sustainable success.

Jung taught that before you can rise, you must first descend. You must turn inward to the spaces where fear lingers, and guilt quietly restrains you. You must confront the hidden beliefs of scarcity and invisibility that still shape your choices. Until these fragments are acknowledged and integrated, your outer world will remain a mirror of the unresolved conflict within.

Each chapter of this book has revealed my investigational findings ranging from naming subconscious patterns to activating archetypal potential, from regulating your nervous system to stepping into symbolic action. Together, they've not only mapped your internal wealth terrain, but they've also unlocked the deeper question of who you are becoming in the process.

To live as your success archetype is not to perform confidence or mimic abundance. It is to embody an aligned, coherent version of you. This is the person who no longer strives to be wealthy but lives as if wholeness itself is wealth.

This transformation is not theoretical, and the archetypes are not metaphors. My investigation has uncovered living codes. They shape your instincts, influence your choices, and mirror your beliefs until you become conscious of them. When you do—the moment you can name the archetype running your wealth patterns—you unlock the power to choose again.

Because, ultimately, your story is not just personal. It's archetypal. When you transform your story, you create a ripple that reaches far beyond your bank account. You impact the field.

This is where you come to the edge of a new paradigm. The old systems and those built on scarcity are going to eventually crumble. They're no longer sufficient for a soul-driven life and Jung once warned that "neurosis is the suffering of a soul that has not discovered its meaning." This collective wealth neurosis has taken the form of burnout bypassing disguised as success. The cure is not to hustle but, rather, to find meaning.

So how do you know you are truly living the Success Archetype? You stop asking, "How do I make more money?" and begin asking, "Who must I become to naturally attract abundance?" Your focus shifts from manipulating outcomes to shaping the kind of presence that creates a new system of opportunity. Gradually, you realize that your deepest wealth does not come from performance or external validation, but it comes from embodiment.

This is the invitation Jung left us. "People who live in symbolic realities are never neurotic," he wrote. When the unconscious is expressed through symbol, it no longer needs to undermine or sabotage. To live symbolically is to allow every financial choice, every client interaction and every investment you make to reflect the coherence and integrity of your inner self. This is not perfection. It is presence. So what now? What happens after the final chapter?

You begin to live the myth. There are three invitations that will carry you forward, not as fixed steps, but as lifelong practices. First, let your wealth serve something larger than you. When you evolve, your wealth must evolve with you. Circulate it and invest in legacies that rewrite the collective story.

Second, continue the inner dialogue with your archetypes. They are not static. They grow with you. Engage with them through journaling, dreamwork, and active Imagination.

Let your psyche keep speaking and, finally, practice integration daily. Track where your actions align or deviate. Watch where fear speaks louder than truth.

Then return, not with shame, but with sovereignty, because to live the success archetype is not to impress the world. It is to embody the self.

Jung once said, "The world hangs by a thin thread, and that thread is the psyche of man."

If we are to create a future where wealth is sacred, sustainable, and soul-aligned, we must begin here with our inner world. This book was never about money. It was about transformation. So, step forward, not with more strategies, but with more soul—not to perform prosperity, but to live it as the archetype, the author, and the self.

Closing Statement:

From an author's perspective, this investigational analysis has taken me on a journey that has forever altered the landscape of my own life. What began as a curiosity and a desire to decode wealth beyond metrics and mechanics soon became a deep psychological excavation.

Each chapter, each archetype, and each shadow that I uncovered has been a mirror. It has become a portal for me—an initiation into a truth that no longer fits inside the limits of conventional thinking.

Writing this book was, for me, a process of making the unconscious conscious and of seeing how much of our relationship with money, power, and success is inherited, conditioned, symbolic, and deeply personal. My goal in these pages was never to offer quick fixes or surface-level strategies. My goal was to open the door, even just slightly, so that others might walk through to wake up to new ideas and new ways of being—a way of living where wealth is not a prize to be earned but a presence to be embodied and where power is not dominance but integration.

So, this is not the end. This is an invitation. You now hold a key, not to my truth, but to your own. With that key, I hope you unlock not just more income or influence, but a deeper intimacy with who you truly are.

Thank you for walking this path with me.

Now, may you walk your own with clarity, sovereignty, and symbolic wealth encoded in every step.

REFERENCES

Bolen, Jean Shinoda. *Goddesses in Everywoman: Powerful Archetypes in Women's Lives.* Harper & Row, 1984.

Campbell, Joseph. *The Hero with a Thousand Faces.* Princeton University Press, 1949.

Dispenza, Joe. *Breaking the Habit of Being Yourself: How to Lose Your Mind and Create a New One.* Hay House, 2012.

Ford, Debbie. *The Dark Side of the Light Chasers.* Riverhead Books, 1998.

Hillman, James. *The Soul's Code: In Search of Character and Calling.* Random House, 1996.

Hopcke, Robert H. *A Guided Tour of the Collected Works of C.G. Jung.* Shambhala Publications, 1989.

Jung, Carl Gustav. *Archetypes and the Collective Unconscious.* Princeton University Press, 1959.

Jung, Carl Gustav. *Memories, Dreams, Reflections.* Vintage Books, 1963.

Jung, Carl Gustav. *Psychological Types.* Princeton University Press, 1921.

Jung, Carl Gustav. *The Red Book: Liber Novus.* W.W. Norton & Company, 2009.

Neumann, Erich. *The Origins and History of Consciousness.* Princeton University Press, 1954.

Pearson, Carol S. *Awakening the Heroes Within: Twelve Archetypes to Help Us Find Ourselves and Transform Our World.* HarperOne, 1991.

Singer, June. *Boundaries of the Soul: The Practice of Jung's Psychology.* Anchor Books, 1972.

Stevens, Anthony. *Jung: A Very Short Introduction.* Oxford University Press, 2001.

Tolle, Eckhart. *A New Earth: Awakening to Your Life's Purpose.* Penguin Group, 2005.

Vogler, Christopher. *The Writer's Journey: Mythic Structure for Writers.* Michael Wiese Productions, 1992.

Wilber, Ken. *The Atman Project: A Transpersonal View of Human Development.* Quest Books, 1980.

Zweig, Connie, and Jeremiah Abrams. *Meeting the Shadow: The Hidden Power of the Dark Side of Human Nature.* TarcherPerigee, 1991.

Buffett, Warren. *The Essays of Warren Buffett: Lessons for Corporate America.* Edited by Lawrence A. Cunningham. Cunningham, 1997.

Buffett, Warren, and David Clark. *Buffettology.* Scribner, 1997.

Case Studies & Media References

Blakely, Sara. *How I Built This* [Audio podcast episode]. Hosted by Guy Raz, NPR, April 17, 2017.
https://www.npr.org/2017/04/17/524447361/sara-blakely-how-i-built-this

Forbes. "How Sara Blakely Turned $5,000 into a Billion-Dollar Company." *Forbes*, June 6, 2012. https://www.forbes.com/sites/jennagoudreau/2012/06/06/sara-blakely-spanx-billionaire

Schultz, Howard. *Onward: How Starbucks Fought for Its Life without Losing Its Soul.* Rodale Books, 2011.

Schultz, Howard, and Dori Jones Yang. *Pour Your Heart into It: How Starbucks Built a Company One Cup at a Time.* Hyperion, 1997.

Winfrey, Oprah. *What I Know for Sure.* Flatiron Books, 2014.

Zakaria, Fareed. "Oprah Winfrey's American Dream." *TIME Magazine*, October 1, 2007. http://content.time.com/time/magazine/article/0,9171,1668459,00.html

ABOUT THE AUTHOR

Jessica Jameson is a first-generation author, wife, and mother whose work explores the intersection of psychology, symbolism, and success. Born and raised in Chicago, she proudly carries the heritage of her Puerto Rican ancestry—a legacy of resilience and vision that shapes her voice and her mission. Bilingual and deeply rooted in her culture, she bridges tradition with transformation, offering readers a unique perspective where practical insight meets timeless wisdom.

Through her writing, Jessica invites readers to open the mind and explore the psyche—woven from beliefs, stories, and symbols—and to step into a life of intentional, soul-aligned success. Both practical and visionary, her work calls readers to redefine success not as the endless pursuit of more, but as the embodiment of purpose and alignment.

www.ingramcontent.com/pod-product-compliance
Lightning Source LLC
Chambersburg PA
CBHW020536030426
42337CB00013B/877